Generous Thinking

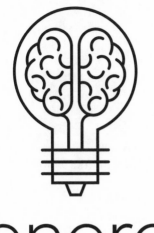

Generous Thinking

A RADICAL APPROACH
TO SAVING
THE UNIVERSITY

KATHLEEN FITZPATRICK

Johns Hopkins University Press
Baltimore

Johns Hopkins University Press
2715 North Charles Street
Baltimore, Maryland 21218-4363
www.press.jhu.edu

Library of Congress Cataloging-in-Publication Data

Names: Fitzpatrick, Kathleen, 1967– author.
Title: Generous thinking : a radical approach to saving the university /
    Kathleen Fitzpatrick.
Description: Baltimore : Johns Hopkins University Press, 2019. | Includes
    bibliographical references and index.
Identifiers: LCCN 2018039680 | ISBN 9781421429465 (hardcover : alk. paper) |
    ISBN 9781421429472 (electronic) | ISBN 1421429462 (hardcover : alk. paper) |
    ISBN 1421429470 (electronic)
Subjects: LCSH: Humanities—Study and teaching (Higher) | Education,
    Higher—Aims and objectives.
Classification: LCC AZ182 . F58 2019 | DDC 378.1/03—dc23
LC record available at https://lccn.loc.gov/2018039680

A catalog record for this book is available from the British Library.

Special discounts are available for bulk purchases of this book. For more information,
please contact Special Sales at 410-516-6936 or specialsales@press.jhu.edu.

Johns Hopkins University Press uses environmentally friendly book
materials, including recycled text paper that is composed of at least
30 percent post-consumer waste, whenever possible.

For Martha, Cris, Rena, Toni, and Val,
models of generous thinking I most needed,
when I most needed them

Our generosity may leave us empty, but our emptiness then pulls gently at the whole until the thing in motion returns to replenish us.—Lewis Hyde, *The Gift*

Contents

Preface

The book you have in front of you explores some possibilities for rebuilding a relationship of trust between universities and the publics they are meant to serve. That this trust—like so much else in today's public sphere—needs rebuilding seems all too evident as I write, in 2018, as the news is filled with evidence of its spectacular failures. The university has been undermined by the withdrawal of public support for its functions, but that public support has been undermined by the university's own betrayals of the public trust. My hope is that this volume might provide one pathway toward renewing that trust. It won't be easy, but it's crucial to the future of higher education—perhaps especially, though not exclusively, in the United States—that we try.

The central argument of this book begins from the growing sense that the critical thinking that forms the center of higher education today has somehow fallen out of whack, that it has come to be seen as privileging the negation rather than creation of ideas and institutions. The problem with this critical mode is not that its insights aren't correct, nor that the structures of contemporary culture don't require critique, but rather, first, that that critique has become less a means of paving the way toward a better alternative than an end in itself, and second, that this mode of critique, of rejection, of refusal has metastasized, becoming the dominant mode of political reaction in recent years. The greatest manifestation of this refusal may well be the pervasive refusal to listen, without which real critical thinking—the contemplation of ideas from multiple points of view, the weighing of evidence for and against, the selection among carefully considered alternatives—is impossible. The mode of critique practiced in academic life certainly does not bear sole responsibility for the devolution of public discourse into an endless series of shouting matches, but the rejection that is so often practiced within the academy—a rejection, as I'll argue, mandated by the competitive structures of reward that shape the contemporary university—has been embraced and indeed perfected by precisely the forces that those academic critics have sought to oppose. If we are to find a way out of this mess, we need to restore the basis of critical thinking by regrounding public discourse in listening, in generosity, in community.

The first seeds of the idea for this book were planted late in the Obama administration, a time when the call to generosity, community, and care seemed only natural, if imperfectly acted upon. Much of it was drafted during the 2016 presidential campaign and its 2017 aftermath, when the same call seemed to take on a kind of desperation. It has been difficult, in several ways, to keep this from becoming a fundamentally angry or despairing book, while nonetheless allowing its anger and despair space in amongst its general emotional swirl. Acknowledging those emotions and their often very personal origins is one of the ways in which this book tries to find some common ground with the public that it seeks to create, a public that is not just composed of other scholars but also administrators, students, parents, policymakers, and the many other people who affect and care about the futures of our institutions of higher education. The book also tries, as much as possible, to minimize its scholarly apparatus; while I still rely on many voices who have contributed significantly to my thinking about the questions I raise, my goal has been to keep this text as broadly accessible as possible.

As is true of any book, this one is of necessity incomplete. It is a snapshot in time, a view from a particular place at a particular moment. It tries to recognize the enormous diversity within the higher education landscape today but is finally grounded in the place where I sit: a large, public, land-grant research university in the United States. I've included a large number of perspectives and examples in thinking through the problems I'm exploring, but there are many other writers and thinkers on higher education today who could have been included. While this book begins from a scholar's concerns and ways of looking at the world—that is inescapably who I am—it doesn't carry with it the scholar's usual desire for completeness. There is much, much more that could be said, and—I'll return to this point in the end—I hope that you'll participate in saying it.

Generous Thinking

Introduction

Community offers the promise of belonging and
calls for us to acknowledge our interdependence. To
belong is to act as an investor, owner, and creator of
this place. To be welcome, even if we are strangers....
To feel a sense of belonging is important because it
will lead us from conversations about safety and
comfort to other conversations, such as our relatedness
and willingness to provide hospitality and generosity.
—PETER BLOCK, *COMMUNITY*

One of the dangers we face in our educational systems is the loss of a feeling of community, not just the
loss of closeness among those with whom we work
and with our students, but also the loss of a feeling of
connection and closeness with the world beyond the
academy.
—BELL HOOKS, *TEACHING COMMUNITY*

The argument that this book presents—and I will admit right
up front that this is an argument and that I am hoping to
persuade you of its rightness—begins for me with what has
come to feel like an emblematic moment of university life. Some
years ago, I gave my graduate seminar a recent article to read. I do
not now remember what that article was, or even what it was
about, but I do remember clearly that upon opening the discussion by asking for first impressions, several students in a row

offered fairly merciless takedowns, pointing out the essay's critical failures and ideological blindspots. Some of those readings were justified, but at least a couple of them seemed, frankly, to have missed the point. After the third such response, I interjected: "Okay, okay, I want to dig into all of that, but let's back up a bit first. What's the author's argument? What's her goal in the article? What does she want the reader to come away with?"

Silence.

I won't rehash all of what ensued, but suffice it to say that it was a difficult moment. I was a lot younger and a fair bit less steady on my feet then, and my initial response to the silence was to start wondering whether I'd asked a stupid question, whether the sudden failure to meet my gaze was a sign that my students were now wondering how I'd ever gotten to this point in my career with such a pedestrian perspective, whether having asked them about the argument was tantamount to asking them what the author's name was and where they might find it on the page, either so painfully obvious that they were mortified to find themselves being treated like high-school students or so apparently superficial that there must be deeper layers that they were missing. "It's not a trick question," I said, asking again for somebody to take a stab at summarizing the argument. It only gradually became clear to me that the question was not stupid or superficial but rather oddly unfamiliar, that everything in their educations to that point had prepared them for interrogating and unpacking, demystifying and subverting, all of the most important critical acts of reading against the grain—what Peter Elbow once called "the doubting game"—but too little emphasis had been placed on its complement, "the believing game," and its central acts of paying attention, of listening, of reading with rather than reading against.

Before this starts to sound like a complaint about the kids these days, let me place alongside it another emblematic anecdote, this one in the form of a Twitter joke:

> *question answered, next dude steps up to mic*
>
> Hi, this is not so much a question and more of a—
>
> *trap door opens, he plummets. Slurping sounds and screams are cut off by the sealing of the floor above him*
>
> *brief hiatus as two-thirds of the line return to their seats* (Baker)

The hilarity that this joke induces has everything to do with our recognition of that moment, the frequency with which we find ourselves in a post-presentation "discussion session" in which there is precious little discussion of the presentation per se and a whole lot more airing of views. It's not that the views are bad, or that comments are unwarranted: rather, this moment indicates something about our dispositions in the act of engaging with the ideas of others, which is to say that they are too often fixated on our own ideas, that we are waiting for the next moment when we can get them on the table.

This book is in large part about my desire to see universities and those who work in and around them—faculty members and administrators, in particular, but also staff members, students, parents, trustees, legislators, and the many other people who affect or are concerned about the futures of our institutions of higher education—develop more responsive, more open, more positive relationships that reach across the borders of our campuses. In it I argue that a key component of building those relationships is for all of us to cultivate a greater disposition toward what I am going to call "generous thinking," a mode of engagement that emphasizes listening over speaking, community over individualism, collaboration over competition, and lingering with the ideas that are in front of us rather than continually pressing forward to where we want to go. But I don't want the two examples above to make it appear that I am primarily focused on getting those of us within the university to communicate more productively with one another, though that certainly wouldn't hurt. The ways that we exchange ideas with one another—in our publications, at our conferences, in our committee meetings—could all bear some close examination. However, in the chapters that follow, I am asking us to take a closer look at the ways that we connect with a range of broader publics around and through our work, publics ranging from our students to our local communities and beyond, to all the ways the university engages with the world. And some focused thinking about that mode of public connection is in order, I would suggest, because our institutions are facing a panoply of crises that we cannot solve on our own.

These crises, I want to acknowledge right at the outset, do not always give the impression of being life-threatening, world-historical, or approaching the kind or degree of the highly volatile political situation spreading around the globe, a moment when the threat of international terrorism is being met with and surpassed by a surge in nationalist politics and domestic terror; when millions of people running for their lives are confused with and held responsible for the thing they're running from; when many residents of our communities find themselves in grave danger posed by those sworn to serve and protect them; when the communications network once imagined to create a borderless utopia of rational collectivist actors not only feeds attacks on those who dare to criticize the manifestations of oppression within that network but also demonstrates its real potential for undermining the constitutional functioning of the nation-state; when the planet itself gives every sign not of nearing an ecological tipping point but, instead, of being well past it.

And yet the decline in public support for higher education is, as Michael Fabricant and Stephen Brier argue in *Austerity Blues*, of a piece with these other crises, part of a series of national and international transformations in assumptions about the responsibility of governments for the public good—the very notion, in fact, that there *can be* such a thing as the public good—and the consequences of those transformations are indeed life or death in many cases.

This connection may not seem obvious. To some readers, no doubt, the fact that at this hour of the world I am writing about the importance of generosity for the future of the university may appear self-indulgent and self-marginalizing, a head-in-the-sand retreat into the aesthetic (or worse, the academic) and a refusal of real political action. I hope, by the end of this book, to have put together a case for why this is not so—why, in fact, the particular modes of generous thinking that I am asking us to undertake within and around our institutions of higher education have the potential to help us navigate the present crises, if not to solve them. Of course, many academic fields are directly focused on pressing public issues, and many scholars are already working in publicly engaged ways. The argument of the book that follows asks us, in some sense, to generalize that engagement, and to think about the ways that it might, if permitted, transform the institution and the ways that scholars, students, and staff members work within it. That is to say, the best of what the university has to offer lies less in its specific power to advance knowledge or solve problems in any of its many fields than in its more general, more crucial ability to be a model and a support for generous thinking as a way of being in and with the world. It's for this reason that those of us who work in those institutions must take a good hard look at ourselves and the ways that we engage with one another and with the world, in order to ensure that we're doing everything we possibly can to create the ways of thinking we'd like to see manifested around us.

Us and Them

But first: Who is this "we" I keep referring to, what is it precisely that we do, and why does it matter? Much of this book focuses on the university's permanent faculty, partially because that faculty is my community of practice and partially because of the extent to which the work done by the faculty is the public face of the university: research and teaching are the primary purposes and visible outputs of our institutions. Moreover, the principles of shared governance under which many of our institutions operate—at least in theory—suggest that tenured and tenure-track faculty members are key contributors to the future of those institutions. Whether through action or neglect, we have helped create the university's present situation, and we need to contend with that, not least by taking responsibility for shaping what is to come. But I want to be careful with the ways that I deploy this "we." As Helen Small has pointed out, "The first person plural is the regularly preferred point of view for much writing about the academic profession for the academic profession. It is a rhetorical sleight of hand by which the concerns of the profession can be made to seem entirely congruent with those of the democratic polity as a whole" (141). That is to say, I hope that the argument that follows has something important to say to readers who teach at institutions of higher education but off the tenure track, or who work on university campuses but are not faculty, or who do not work on university campuses at all, and that it might become possible for the "we" that I am addressing to refer to all of us, on campus and off, who want to strengthen both our systems of higher education and our ways of engaging with one another in order to help us all build stronger, more empowered communities. But it's important to acknowledge that the "we" that bears the greatest responsibility for caring for the university and for building relationships between the university and the broader publics that it serves, and thus the most immediate antecedent for my "we," is those of us on campus, and especially the permanent faculty.

Every "we" implies a "them," of course, and the ways we define and conceive of that "them" points to one of the primary problems of the contemporary university, and especially the public university in the United States. These institutions were founded explicitly to serve the people of their states or regions or communities, and thus those publics should be understood as part of "us." And yet, the borders of the campus have done more than define a space: they determine a sense of belonging as well, transforming everything off-campus into "them," a generalized other. We recognize that they are, in varying ways, people with whom we want to engage, but it's important to consider how, given the ways that our interactions will inevitably be defined by the ways we think of those with whom we interact. As Kelly Susan Bradbury has explored, traditional academics' exclusion of certain kinds of education and certain kinds of work from the category of the "intellectual" profoundly affects nonacademics' willingness to understand themselves as part of that category, and the rampant anti-intellectualism in American culture may well be a result, a defensive reaction against what is felt to be a prior exclusion. That is to say, academics' presumed authority over who gets to be an intellectual comes with a profound cost, as it convinces "them" that they are not, and that they would not want to be.

So it's important for us to ask ourselves: Do we understand the people who are not on campus to be an audience—a passive group that merely takes in information that the university provides? Do we understand them to be a public, a self-activated and actualized group capable not only of participating in multidirectional exchanges both with the university and among its members, but also of acting on its own behalf? Or even more, do we consider them to be a complex collection of communities—not just groups who interact with one another and with us, but groups of which we are in fact a part? How can we shape this understanding in a way that might begin to create a richer, more interactive, more generous sense not just of "them" but of the larger "us" that we together form?

Such an understanding requires some careful thinking about the nature of community, which is a thornier concept than it might at first appear. As Miranda Joseph writes in *Against the Romance of Community*, the concept is often used as a placeholder for something that exists outside the dominant institutional structures of contemporary life, a set of ostensibly organic felt relationships that derive from a mythical premodern moment in which people lived and worked in more direct connection with one another, without the mediating forces of modern capitalism. "Community" is also an imagined relationship, in Benedict Anderson's sense, as its invocation is designed to yoke together bodies whose existence as a group is largely constructed. "The gay community" serves in this fashion as Joseph's primary reference point, a concept often used both idealistically and as a form of discipline, a claim of unity that smooths over and thus suppresses internal difference and disagreement.

Moreover, Joseph points out, the notion of community is often deployed as if the relationships that it describes could provide an antidote to or an escape from the problems created by contemporary political and economic life. This suggestion, she argues, serves to distract us from the supplementary role that community actually serves with respect to the mainstream economy, filling its gaps and smoothing over its flaws in ways that permit it to function without real opposition. The alternative presented by community—people working together! helping each other!—allows the specter of socialism, or genuine state support for the needs of the public, to be dismissed. Thus we turn to social network–based fundraising campaigns to support people facing major health crises, rather than demanding universal health care. Thus elementary school bake sales rather than full funding for education. And thus a wide range of activity among nonprofit organizations—entities that often describe themselves explicitly as working on behalf of the community—that serve to fill needs left behind by a retreating state and thereby allow that retreat to go unchallenged.

As Fabricant and Brier explore in *Austerity Blues,* the state's ongoing disclaimer of its responsibilities for the public welfare, from the Reagan era forward, makes itself felt across the social sphere—in housing policy, in environmental policy, and, of course, in education. Throughout this book, one of my interests lies in the effects of, and the need to reverse, the shift in our cultural understanding of education, and especially higher education; where in the mid-twentieth century, the value of education was largely understood to be social, it has in recent decades come to be described as providing primarily private, individual benefits. And this, inevitably, has accompanied a shift from education being treated as a public service to being treated as a private responsibility. Fabricant and Brier note that this transition is just one manifestation of the state gradually displacing its responsibilities for the public welfare onto private citizens and, as Joseph's reading suggests, onto a range of socially oriented nonprofits supported largely through private philanthropy. This displacement is at work in the defunding of public universities, which effectively transforms them into nonprofit organizations rather than state institutions. The effects of this program of neoliberal reform run deep, not least being that the dominant motivator behind these privatized institutions becomes sustainability rather than service, leaving universities, like nonprofits, in an endless cycle of fundraising and budget cuts.

The argument in favor of privatization's displacement of responsibility for the public good from the state to the community, one largely accepted on both sides of the aisle, is in significant part based on the inefficiency of government bureaucracies and the far more streamlined and therefore ostensibly effective practices made possible in the private sector. Reversing the trend toward privatization will thus require not just massive public mobilization and demand of elected officials, but also a hard turn away from efficiency as a primary value, and thus a recognition that the building of relationships and the cultivation of care are slow and difficult and of necessity inefficient. In fact, that the value of the public good lies precisely in the ways that it refuses efficiency— but making the case for such a refusal as a necessary value requires a lot of effort, and a lot of caution. My hope is that *Generous Thinking* might lay some key groundwork for that case.

Similar caution is necessary in the calls to "community" that this book issues: such calls, issued uncritically, not only run the risk of enabling the institutions that structure contemporary life to absolve themselves of responsibility for public care, but they also risk essentializing a highly complex and intersectional set of social relations, treating those relations as if they were a simple, single thing. One key aspect of the problem with "the community," that is, might be less about "community" than about "the"; it's possible that acknowledging and foregrounding the multiple and multifarious communities with which all of us engage might help us avoid the exclusions that the declaration of groupness is often designed to produce, the "us" that inevitably suggests a "them." My hope is that my uses of the notion of community throughout this book might benefit from a variant on Gayatri Spivak's "strategic essentialism," a recognition that our definitions of community are always reductive, but also at least potentially useful as organizing tools. In this sense, "community" might serve not to evoke a dangerous, mythical notion of organic unity, but instead a form of solidarity, of coalition-building.

The pragmatic coalition-building function of community is crucial to the future of the university, both in its understanding of the publics with which the institution might work and in its understanding of its own internal structure. But it's also a key part of the university's recent past, one of the important elements of its history that have been undone by recent political shifts. The potential for connecting the university to the communities around it drove student-led calls for institutional change in the 1960s and 1970s, and the understanding of the coalition-building potential of community has long been central to women of color feminisms. But these are calls that have not only gone unheeded but that have in fact been actively countered. Roderick Ferguson, in *We Demand,* presents a stark portrait of the history of administration and government responses to student and social movements, noting that the dismantling of the public university's publicness begins with a rejection of the expansion of the publics those institutions were intended to serve. Viewed in this light, the Reagan-era launch of the defunding of higher education stems from this backlash against student protests. As Ferguson argues, "Neoliberalism is not just an economic and political formation involving governments and businesses but an ideological project meant to tear down the web of insurgencies that activists have been demanding" (69). The economic in this sense becomes a tool for undoing the political: the state begins its withdrawal from responsibility for the public good at the point at which minoritized communities become inescapably part of the public. This may not be a simple matter of cause and effect, although, as Ferguson explores, the 1971 Powell memorandum's work to argue that corporations, rather than people of color, are the real victims of marginalization certainly indicates a more than casual connection between the neoliberal willingness to tear down the welfare state and all its trappings, including public education, and the recognition of the growing power of minoritized communities.

In this sense, community is and has been the university's weakness, when it should have been its strength. Community has been framed as a site of tension, beginning with the legendary town/gown divide and continuing through anxieties about student activism, when it should have been a source of potential. If we—those of us both on campus and off interested in the project of saving the university both from its opponents and from itself— attempt to understand community strategically, we might be able to build some new collaborations that can help support the university's future. Recognizing that community is something that does not simply exist but instead must be built, recognizing that community is always complex, negotiated, multifarious, and recognizing the forces that are arrayed against the formation of community might help institutions of higher education, and all of us that work within and for them, think differently about what we do and how we do it. If we were able to understand the university both internally and in its outward connections not as a giant nonprofit organization, focused on the fiscal sustainability required to provide services to a generically understood public, but instead as a site of voluntary community—a site of solidarity— forged with and by the publics we seek to engage, we might begin to develop new models, new structures, that could help all of us reconnect with and recommit to a sense of the common good.

The Liberal Arts

However, in building such a strategic sense of community, we need to contend with the fact that what faculty members actually do on our campuses is often a mystery, and indeed a site of profound misunderstanding, for people outside the academic profession, and even at times for one another. One of my goals in this book is to open our work up a bit, to make the what and why of some parts of university life a bit less opaque, and to encourage all of us to continue that project in ways that might help build a much better sense of the importance of the university in the contemporary world. One of the key areas of misconception about the university today, and one that most needs opening up, is its fundamental purpose. There is, of course, more than one such purpose that these institutions serve: as Clark Kerr said in his 1963 Godkin Lectures at Harvard, universities might be more appropriately called "multiversities," containing as they do "a whole series of communities and activities held together by a common name [and] a common governing board" (1). And of course there are many different kinds of universities, including elite privates, flagship publics, and regional comprehensives, not to mention small liberal arts colleges and community colleges, all of which have different focuses and different purposes. But when we come down to the central question of why we should *have* a university, or why you should *attend* one, we hit a core difference of opinion.

Public figures such as politicians, trustees, and accrediting bodies increasingly focus on the university as a site of workforce preparation—which, of course, it is: the educations provided by the range of institutions that fall under the category of "universities" provide crucial skills and credentials that enable students to engage in productive careers. However, these discussions often make it sound as if that were the only important part of the university's role, as if the provision of career-enhancing credentials were the sole purpose for which our institutions exist, and as if everything else they do that does not lead directly to economic growth were—especially in the case of public institutions—a misappropriation of resources. This is a pernicious assumption, one that has spread through public discourse and become widely adopted by parents and students, with profound effects on the ways they approach their investments in and time at the university.

Those of us who work in universities, however—the faculty in particular, but also many administrators and a good number of students—think of our institutions not as credentialing agencies but as sites of broad-based education. Thus we might see Chad Wellmon's turn to the notion of "the academy," by which he means the collection of "activities, practices, goals, and norms related to the creation, cultivation, and transmission of knowledge," as an entity that risks being subsumed by the bureaucratic structures of the university and that must, in his view, be defended from it. The academy in Wellmon's sense is a community capable of providing the deepest, richest possible education, a liberal education in the original sense of the term.

Of course the very label of "liberal education" today, so natural to those of us who are engaged in it, has itself become profoundly politicized, leading the University of Colorado's board of regents to contemplate removing the term "liberal" from the institution's governing documents, as if the liberal aspect of the education it provides were not its breadth but its ideological bent (Zahneis). This politicization has led to some of the most entrenched assumptions and accusations about what's happening on campus these days. Universities are seen by the Right as excluding conservative perspectives and as coddling their liberal snowflake students—claims that, as Ferguson demonstrates, have long been used to demean and thus defuse student movements and to ensure the continued dominance of the status quo precisely by suggesting it is under threat. In response to these suggestions, ostensibly left-leaning faculty and fields are being explicitly targeted by conservative groups such as Turning Point USA, which are determined to see those faculty and fields silenced, terminated, driven off-campus. But even where revolution isn't imagined to be breeding and in need of being stamped out on university campuses, there's a widespread conception about what we do that's almost worse: we waste taxpayer resources by developing, disseminating, and filling our students' heads with useless knowledge that will not lead to a productive career path, and—this part is true, but for reasons that the university alone cannot control—we leave them in massive debt in the process.

And nowhere is this misconception more focused than on the humanities. The humanities are of course only a subset of the constellation of fields that together form the liberal arts, the core academic disciplines that, rather than providing direct professional training, instead engage students through a broad grounding in the study of the cultural, social, and natural world. The liberal arts thus include the sciences and social sciences, though the term has come to be somewhat overidentified with the humanities, whose fields include history, literature, languages, art history, philosophy, and so on—the least pre-professional of the non-pre-professional. Given that relationship, the portrait I'm about to sketch of the humanities today could be extended to many other areas within the curriculum; for example, the sciences' focus on "basic science," or science without direct industry applicability, is often imagined to be just as useless. But the humanities are in certain ways both the core and the limit case of the liberal arts. These fields cultivate an inquisitive mindset, they teach key skills of reading and interpretation, and they focus on writing in ways that can prepare students to learn absolutely anything else over the course of their lives. As the National Humanities Alliance argues in their toolkit on making the case for studying the humanities, the skills these fields foster are highly desired by employers, and humanities majors outperform their peers in several important ways—and yet the humanities are the fields around which no end of jokes about what a student might actually *do* with that degree have been constructed. (The answer is embedded above: *absolutely anything*. In fact, as Derek Newton explores in a blog post for *Forbes*, the majors that a recent study suggests result in the greatest chance of underemployment are those that seem least likely: "Business, Management, Marketing, and Related Support Services." Moreover, as the American Academy of Arts and Sciences *Humanities Indicators* project demonstrates, not only do humanities majors end up gainfully employed, but their job satisfaction is among the highest. In other words, they are *happy* in what they do. But I digress.) In this dismissal of the humanities as a collection of valuable fields of study, they serve as a bellwether: what has been happening to them is happening to the university in general, if a little more slowly. So while I focus in some parts of what's ahead on the kinds of arguments that are being made about the humanities in our culture today, it doesn't take too much of a stretch to imagine them being made about sociology, or about physics, or about any other field on campus that isn't named after a specific, remunerative career.

The humanities, in any case, have long been lauded as providing students with a rich set of interpretive, critical, and ethical skills with which they can engage the world around them. These reading, thinking, and writing skills are increasingly necessary in today's hypermediated, globalized, conflict-filled world—and yet many humanities departments feel themselves increasingly marginalized within their own institutions. This marginalization is related, if not directly attributable, to the degree to which students, parents, administrators, trustees, politicians, the media, and the public at large have been led in a self-reinforcing cycle to believe that these fields are a luxury in the current economic environment: someone particularly visible makes a publicly disparaging remark about what students are going to do with all those art-history degrees; commentators reinforce the sense that humanities majors are worth less than pre-professional degrees with the presumption of clearly defined career paths; parents strongly encourage their students to turn toward fields that seem more pragmatic in such economically uncertain times, fields that seem somehow to describe a job; administrators note a decline in humanities majors and cut budgets and positions; the jobs crisis for humanities PhDs worsens; the media notices; someone particularly visible makes a publicly disparaging remark about what all those adjuncts were planning on doing with that humanities PhD anyhow; and the whole thing intensifies. In many institutions, this draining away of majors and faculty and resources has reduced the humanities to a means of ensuring that students studying to become engineers and bankers are reminded of the human ends of their work. This is not a terrible thing in and of itself—David Silbersweig has written compellingly in the *Washington Post* about the importance that his undergraduate philosophy major has had for his career as a neuroscientist—but it is not a sufficient ground on which humanities fields can thrive as fields, with their own educational aims, their own research problems, and their own values and goals.

And while this kind of cyclical crisis has not manifested to anything like the same extent in the sciences, there are early indications that it may be spreading in that direction. Concerns around the need to preserve and protect basic research in an era driven by more applied, capitalizable outcomes and beset by the conviction that science has developed a leftward ideological bent are increasing. Where we might once have assumed that the world at large mostly understands that scientific research and the kinds of study that support it are crucial to the general advancement of knowledge, recent shifts in funder policies and priorities suggest a growing scrutiny of that work's economic rather than educational impact, as well as a growing restriction on research areas that have been heavily politicized. Again, the humanities may well be the canary in the university's coal mine, and for that reason, it's crucial that those concerned about the university's future pay close attention to what's happened in those fields, and particularly to the things that haven't worked as the humanities have attempted to remedy the situation.

One of the key things that hasn't worked is the impassioned plea on behalf of humanities fields: a welter of defenses of the humanities from both inside and outside the academy has been published in recent years, each of which has seemed slightly more defensive than the last, and none of which has had the desired impact. Calls to save the humanities issued by public figures have frequently left scholars dissatisfied, as they often begin with an undertheorized and perhaps even somewhat retrograde sense of what we do and why, and thus frequently give the sense of trying to save our fields from us. (I might here gesture toward a column published in 2016 by the former chairman of the National Endowment for the Humanities, Bruce Cole, entitled "What's Wrong with the Humanities?", which begins memorably: "Let's face it: Too many humanities scholars are alienating students and the public with their opacity, triviality, and irrelevance.") But perhaps even worse is the degree to which humanities professors themselves—those who, one would think, are best positioned to make the case—have failed to find traction with their arguments. As the unsuccessful defenses proliferate, the public view of the humanities becomes all the worse, leading Simon During to grumble that "whatever things the humanities do well, it is beginning to look as if promoting themselves is not among them." One would be justified in wondering whether, in fact, humanities scholars like it that way, as we are often those who take issue with our own defenses, bitterly disagreeing as we frequently do about the purposes and practices of our fields.

Perhaps this is a good moment for us to stop and consider what it is that the humanities do do well, what the humanities are for. I will start with a basic definition of the humanities as a cluster of fields that focus on the careful study and analysis of cultures and their many modes of thought and forms of representation—writing, music, art, media, and so on—as they have developed and moved through time and across geographical boundaries, growing out of and adding to our senses of who we are as individuals, as groups, and as nations. The humanities are interested, then, in the ways that representations work, in the relationships between representations and social structures, and in all the ways that human ideas and their expression shape and are shaped by human culture. In this definition we might begin to see the possibility that studying literature or history or art or film or philosophy might not be solely about the object itself, but instead about a way of engaging with the world: in the process one develops the ability to read and interpret what one sees and hears, the insight to understand the multiple layers of what is being communicated and why, and the capacity to put together for oneself an appropriate, thoughtful contribution.

Now, the first thing to note about this definition is that I am certain that many of the humanities scholars who read it are going to disagree with it—they will have nuances and correctives to offer—and it is important to understand that this disagreement does not necessarily mean that my definition is wrong. Nor do I mean to suggest that the nuances and correctives presented would be wrong. Rather, that disagreement is at the heart what we do: we hear one another's interpretations (of texts, of performances, of historical events), and we push back against them. We advance the work in our fields in part through disagreement and revision. This mode of engagement, which one might reasonably call "agonistic," is more pronounced in some fields than others—philosophy is especially known for being downright pugilistic—but it's common across the humanities and social sciences. Either way, this agonistic approach is both a strength of those fields—and by extension of the university in general—and their Achilles' heel, a thought to which I'll return shortly.

For the moment, though, back to Simon During and his sense that the humanities are terrible at self-promotion. During's complaint, levied at the essays included in Peter Brooks and Hilary Jewett's volume, *The Humanities and Public Life,* is largely that in the act of self-defense, humanities scholars leave behind doing what they do and instead turn to "sermonizing" about the value of what they do. He argues that part of the problem is the assumption that the humanities as we practice them—the study of culture, rather than the objects of culture themselves—ought to have a public life in the first place. For During, it is simply the nature of things that these fields of study "form a world more than they provide a social good," and that making the case for ourselves and our work in "more modest terms" may help us direct that case to "those who matter most in this context": the students who might be inclined to study our fields and the policymakers who might be inclined to support them. In part, During's interest in asking the humanities to stop defending themselves is tied to his sense that these fields—or at least what he refers to as the "core humanities," which I take to mean the study of the canon within the long-established fields of English, history, philosophy, and the like—are intimately implicated in the maintenance rather than the disruption of class- and race-based hierarchies, whose unearned privilege may be one reason why, he notes, these fields have become less popular. He argues in the end that we should remain concerned about ensuring that there is sufficient state support for the humanities in order for students who do not already occupy a position of financial comfort to study our fields, but that we should not stretch beyond that point by insisting on the public importance of studying the humanities, because that importance is primarily, overwhelmingly, private.

This sense that education in the humanities is of primarily private value is everywhere in today's popular discourse extended to higher education in general: the purpose, we are told, of a college degree is some form of personal enrichment, whether financial (a credential that provides access to more lucrative careers) or otherwise (an experience that provides access to useful or satisfying forms of cultural capital). This privatization of higher education's benefits—part of the general privatization that Christopher Newfield has referred to as the academy's "great mistake"—has been accompanied by a similar shift in its costs from the state to individual families and students, resulting in the downward spiral in funding and other forms of public support in which our institutions and our fields are caught, as well as the astronomically increasing debt load faced by students and their families. As long as a university education is assumed to have a predominantly personal rather than social benefit, it will be argued that making such an education possible is a private rather than a public responsibility, one among many such responsibilities that have devolved upon individuals and families as the state has abjured its responsibility for the public well-being under the new economy. And that economistic mindset will of necessity lead to the devaluation of fields whose benefits are less immediately tangible, less material, less individual. If we are to correct course, if we are to restore public support for our institutions and our fields, we must find ways to communicate and to make clear the public goals that our fields have, and the public good that our institutions serve.

But what are those public goals? What are the less tangible benefits of our fields? We don't do a very good job of articulating these things. In fact, despite the role so many of us have as professors, we often seem to have a hard time *professing*, describing what we do and arguing on behalf of the values that sustain our work. It's not unlikely that this difficulty with positive arguments is related to our quite considered rejection of positivism, the philosophical principle that the only valid forms of knowledge are those that are derived from neutral observation and thus objective; we are too aware of the inevitable subjectivity of all observation and all knowledge to take a forceful, public stand on behalf of *our* knowledge. It's hard to express our values without recourse to what feel to us like politically regressive, universalizing master narratives about the nature of the good. And like During, many of us are less than comfortable with making the case to the public for the importance of our work precisely because of the extent to which our fields have been used to define and support cultural and social hierarchies. Such is certainly true of the humanities and the long history of unearned privilege that those fields have stored up, studied, and transmitted: the relationship between the "core humanities" and now-discredited white male–dominated forms of humanism creates grave discomfort for us as we attempt to explain the value of those fields today. Humanism's triumphant belief in the power of human reason and the humanities' study of what Matthew Arnold so blithely but searingly referred to as "the best that has been thought and said" have together long been used as a means of solidifying and perpetuating the social order, with all its injustices and exclusions. We are understandably queasy about our fields' development out of the projects of nationalism and cultural dominance, and we recognize the ways that the fervent expression of values and ideologies has been used to create those projects and all their hierarchies and violences, thereby leaving us unable, unwilling, or just plain nervous about stating clearly and passionately any ethics and values and goals that we bring to our work. We instead protect ourselves with what Lisa Ruddick has described as "the game of academic cool": in order to avoid appearing naïve—or worse, complicit—we complicate; we argue from a rigorously theorized position on behalf of a progressive, and at times radical, project; we read, as they say, against the grain.

That description is no doubt an overgeneralization, and describing our more serious attempts to question the ideological structures of our field as a mere attempt to avoid appearing naïve is uncharitable, if not downright unfair. But it is an intellectual strategy that I think many of us can recognize. More importantly, it's a strategy that in public discourse gets mistaken—at times, it seems, intentionally—for itself being ideological in intent and effect; this is how universities come to be accused of "brainwashing" their students, filling their heads with leftist rejections of the basic goodness of the dominant Western culture. On campus, we know that's not the case: the overwhelming majority of what we teach, even in the most progressively oriented departments, is still that culture. Our classes on Shakespeare, on European art, on American history are still full. It's just that we attempt to teach all of this in context: Shakespeare no longer sits alone atop the canon of literature in English, but is accompanied by authors from around the world; courses on European art consider its deep transnational correspondences and influences; our narrative of American history strives not to leave out the inconveniently ugly bits. It's of course important to recognize the extent to which this scrutiny of the curriculum, and the dismissal of the contemporary humanities as nonserious, coincides with the inclusion of material relevant to minoritized communities, and it's vital to recognize the political (rather than aesthetic) underpinnings of the desire for return to the hierarchies of old-school humanities, most starkly visible in the ways that calls to that cultural heritage have recently been deployed in support of nationalist and white supremacist projects (Perry).

But there's more at work in the strategies with which we argue within our fields than opposition to such regressive, oppressive ideologies; we don't read against the grain just because we reject the politics of the past, or the politics of the present for that matter. In fact, our most critical reading practices are not just a manifestation of our political opposition, but are actually perfectly compatible with the contemporary status quo. As Marco Roth has pointed out, there's an "uncomfortable truth" in the fact that the most critical methods of literary and cultural analysis "have flourished in our period of triumphant neoliberalism, both within the university system and in the world at large." And so the suggestion of a scholar like Winfried Fluck that early twenty-first century problems in the humanities in the United States were tied to "a constant pressure to outradicalize others" (348), especially under the banner of "difference," seems to just miss the mark. The point is not that our critiques surface thanks to pressure from some left-leaning bias in the academy. Rather, the point is that the critiques surface *because of* the conservative-leaning systems and structures in which the university as a whole, and each of us as a result, is mired. Our tendency to read against the grain is part of our makeup precisely because of the ways that we are ourselves *subject to* politics rather than being able to stand outside and neutrally analyze the political. The politics we are subject to, however—and this is the part of Fluck's argument that I think is crucial—is the politics that structures all institutions in the contemporary United States, and perhaps especially universities, a politics that makes inevitable the critical, the negative, the rejection of everything that has gone before. It is a politics structured around market-based competition, and what Fluck refers to as the race for individual distinction.

Critique and Competition

However much we as scholars might reject individualism as part and parcel of the humanist, positivist ways of the past, our working lives—on campus and off—are overdetermined by it. The entire academic enterprise serves to cultivate individualism, in fact. Beginning with college applications, extending through graduate school admissions, fellowship applications, the job market, publication submissions, and, seemingly finally, the tenure and promotion review, those of us on campus are subject to selection. These processes present themselves as meritocratic: there are some metrics for quality against which applicants are measured, and the best—whatever that might mean in a given context—are rewarded. In actual practice, however, those metrics are never neutral, and what we are measured against is far more often than not one another—sometimes literally: it's not uncommon for research universities to ask external reviewers in tenure and promotion cases to rank candidates against the best two or three scholars in the field. Of course, as Erik Simpson reminds me, this kind of request *is* uncommon in other types of institutions, especially community colleges and regional comprehensive universities. And yet that very distinction raises the question of rankings and hierarchies among institutions and institutional types, and the ways that they are required to compete for faculty and other resources. Always, always, in the hidden unconscious of the profession, there is this competition: for positions, for people, for resources, for acclaim. And the drive to compete that this mode of being instills in us can't ever be fully contained by these specific processes; it bleeds out into all areas of the ways we work, even when we're working together. The competitive individualism that the academy cultivates makes all of us painfully aware that even our most collaborative efforts will be assessed individually, with the result that even those fields whose advancement depends most on team-based efforts are required to develop careful guidelines for establishing credit and priority.

This competitive individualism contradicts—and in fact undermines—all of the most important communal aspects of life within our institutions of higher education. Our principles of shared governance, for instance, are built on the notion that colleges and universities operate best as collectives, in which all members contribute to their direction and functioning. In actual practice, however, our all-too-clear understanding that (especially at research universities) service to the institution will have the least impact when we are evaluated and ranked for salary increases and promotions encourages faculty members to avoid that labor, to reserve our time and energy for those aspects of our work that will enable recognition of our individual achievements. The results are not good for any of us: faculty disengage from the functioning of the institution and the shared purposes that it serves; some of the work that we might have done is instead taken on by academic and administrative staff; university governance becomes increasingly an administrative function, with an ever-growing phalanx of associate vice provosts creating and overseeing the processes that structure our institutions and our work within them, ostensibly freeing the faculty up to focus on the competitive work that will allow us as individuals and our universities as institutions to climb the rankings.

This is no way to run a collective. It's also no way to structure a fulfilling life: as I've written elsewhere, this disengagement from community and singular focus on the race for individual distinction is a key factor in the extremely high risk of burnout among college faculty and other intellectual workers. It is all but impossible for us to structure our lives around the things that are most in line with our deepest personal values when we are driven to focus on those things that will create distinction for us, that will allow us to compare ourselves—or our institutions—favorably with one another.

This individualistic, competitive requirement is inseparable from the privatization that Newfield describes as the political unconscious of the contemporary university. Competition and the race for individual distinction structure the growing conviction that not only the benefits of higher education but also all of our categories of success (both in educational outcomes and in intellectual achievement) can only ever be personal, private, individual rather than social. And no amount of trying to persuade ourselves, or our administrations, or our legislatures of the public good that we, our fields, and our institutions serve will take root unless we figure out how to step off the competitive track, to live the multiplicity of our academic lives in ways that diverge from the singular path now laid out before us.

The need for a different way of being extends to all aspects of scholars' lives, including—to return to the agonistic approach to advancing knowledge in the humanities that I mentioned earlier—our critical methodologies. This sense of agon, or struggle, encourages us to reject the readings and arguments that have gone before us and to focus on advancing new ways of looking at the material we study. It is this mode of argumentation that leads Fluck to posit a pressure to "outradicalize" one another, given the need to distinguish ourselves and our readings from the many others in our fields. However, the political orientation of our critiques is ultimately of lesser importance than the competitive drive that lies beneath them. Distinguishing our arguments from those of others working in our fields is the primary goal; that we often choose the terrain of the ideological, or wind up embroiled in what Paul Ricoeur describes as the "hermeneutics of suspicion" in order to effect that distinction is a mere by-product. So when my graduate students began their engagement with the article I'd asked them to read by critiquing—and in fact dismissing—it on ideological grounds, the key force at work was not just what Rita Felski describes in *The Limits of Critique* as our suspicious "conviction" that both the texts that we study and the ways that we have been led to study them are "up to no good" (58). Far more important to the problem in that moment was that my students had no other position than the critical available to them, that the need to stake out their own individual, distinctive positions within the seminar room left them unable to articulate in any positive sense what the article was trying to accomplish because that articulation would have left their own readings somehow indistinguishable from those of the author. So they—we—reject, dismiss, critique. We outradicalize, but in the service of a highly individualistic form of competition. And however much this mode of reading has done to advance our fields and their social commitments—and I will stipulate that it has done a lot—competitive engagement like this too often looks to the many readers just outside our scholarly circles, including students, parents, administrators, and policymakers, like pure negativity, a rejection of the materials of our shared if contested culture, not to mention a seemingly endless series of internal arguments, all of which might well lead them to ask what is to be gained from supporting a field, or an institution, that seems intent on self-dismantling.

Worse, scholars' internalization of the individualistic impera-tive to compete and its manifestation in arguments whose primary work is that of rejection have provided an inroad into higher ed-ucation for some forces that are hastening its dismantling. Bill Readings, in *The University in Ruins,* powerfully traces the transi-tion of the purposes of higher education from the propagation of the culture of the nation-state and the training of its citizens therein, through an important period of resistance and protest that did the crucial work of opening up both access to higher ed-ucation and the canon that it taught, to its current role, which seems to be the production of value (both intellectual and human) for global capital. This is to say that many of our concerns about and critiques of the goals of our institutions of higher learning as they were established are well-founded: they were developed in order to cultivate a particular model of citizenship based on exclusion and oppression and focused on the reproduction of state power. The problem is that in the absence of those defining goals, the purpose of higher education has drifted, and not in the ways we would have hoped. As in so many other areas of the con-temporary public world, where service to the state is no longer focal, and where the state's responsibilities to its citizens are no longer clear, corporate interests have interceded. We may no longer promote exclusion and oppression in training state citizens, but we reinstantiate it in a new guise when we turn, however in-advertently, to training corporate citizens. Even worse, rejecting or critiquing that purpose is simply not working: not only is capi-tal extraordinarily able to absorb all critique and to marginalize those who make it, but our inability to stop competing with one another ensures that our critique is contained within the forces of the market that we serve. Perhaps we might have reached, as Felski's title suggests, the limits of critique; perhaps we might need to adopt a new mode of approach in order to make a dent in the systems that hem us in.

But that is not to say that I am rejecting critique, or critical thinking, or that I think scholars need somehow to find a way "beyond" critique. In fact, the critical approach is at the heart of what scholars do. Not only would we be justified in bristling against any suggestion that we abandon critique, or abandon the social commitments that underwrite it, in favor of an approach to our work that might be more friendly or positive, but we'd also be well within reason if we were to point out that the critique of critique *is still critique,* that it makes use of criticism's negative mode in the very act of negating it. Moreover, the critique of critique is too often driven either by a disdain for difficulty or by a rejection of the political in scholarly work. Scholars, perhaps unsurprisingly, take the rejection of the political critique that grounds our work, often accompanied by calls to return to the traditions that made "Western culture" great, as further evidence of our basic correctness: see, contemporary culture really is dominated by conservative and even reactionary forces that must exclude our ideas as a threat to their very being. We also take the resistance to difficulty, especially in the humanities, whether of language or of argument, as a sign of dismissal, of a refusal to take us and our work seriously: no one, after all, scoffs at the uses of jargon in high-energy physics. Meanwhile, even the physicists scoff at the uses of jargon in the humanities: one might be reminded of Alan Sokal's hoax perpetrated on the journal *Social Text,* in which he submitted an article arguing that gravity is a social construct as a means of demonstrating what he saw as the intellectual vacuity of both the journal and its field. It worked: not only was the article published, but it made cultural studies a laughing stock. Jennifer Ruark explores the cascading impact of this hoax in a recent oral history, in which Sokal himself notes the "persistent anti-intellectual current" in American culture, which "looks down on the pointy-headed professors and is happy to pick up on any excuse to have a laugh at them," recognizing the damage done by this intramural finger-pointing.

None of this is to say that scholars shouldn't be critical of one another's work. It is, however, to suggest that the motives behind our critique might be worth a closer look. And so, too, are the motives behind what feels to us like the public rejection or dismissal of the kinds of work that we do, which might at times be more complex than we automatically assume. For instance, the calls for comprehensibility and the return to tradition in the humanities— see again Bruce Cole—aren't just about a refusal of difficulty, or a refusal to take us and our work seriously. These calls may be at least in part a sign of the degree to which people care about our subject matter, about literature or history or art. They might indicate the degree to which people feel the cultures we study to be their own, leading them to want on some level to engage with us, to understand and participate in what we're up to. If so, a bit of generosity on our part might do much to defuse some of the hostility toward our ways of working. There is of course grave political opposition to much of the work that is done on our college campuses today, and I do not at all wish to dismiss the threat that opposition can pose, but I also want to suggest that that glimmer of care for our subject matter creates the opportunity, if we take it seriously, to create forms of connection and dialogue that might help further rather than stymie the work that we do.

Some of my thinking about ways that attention to care might encourage scholars to approach the work that we do from a slightly different perspective has developed out of a talk I heard a couple of years ago by David Scobey, then the dean of the New

School for Public Engagement. His suggestion was that scholarly work in the humanities is in a kind of imbalance, that critical thinking has dominated at the expense of a more socially directed mode of what he called "generous thinking," and that a recalibration of the balance between the two might enable us to make possible a greater public commitment in our work, which in turn might inspire a greater public commitment to our work. This book, having drawn its title from Scobey, obviously builds on his argument, but with one key revision: generous thinking is not and should not be opposed to critical thinking. In fact, the two should be fully aligned, and my hope in what follows is to help guide us toward modes of working that allow us to more fruitfully connect the generous and the critical in scholarly work. Rather than critical thinking, the dark opposite of generous thinking, that which has in fact created an imbalance in scholarly work—and not just in the humanities, but across the curriculum—is *competitive* thinking, thinking that is compelled by what sociologist and economist Thorstein Veblen called "invidious comparison," or what Fluck refers to as the "race for professional distinction." It is the competitive that has undermined the capacity for community-building, both within our campuses and between our campuses and the broader public. What kinds of new discussions, new relationships, new projects might be possible if our critical thinking practices eschewed competition and were instead grounded in generosity?

Generous Thinking

What is it I mean when I talk about generosity in this context? I'll dig much further into this in the next chapter, but for the moment: I don't mean the term to refer to "giving" in any material sense, or even in any simple metaphorical sense. Instead, what I'm hoping to develop, in myself most of all, is a generosity of mind, by which I mean to indicate an openness to possibility. That openness begins for me by trying to develop a listening presence in the world, which is to say a conversational disposition that is not merely waiting for my next opportunity to speak but instead genuinely focusing on what is being said to me, beginning from the assumption that in any given exchange I likely have less to teach than I have to learn. Generous thinking also means working to think *with* rather than *against,* whether the objects of those prepositions are texts or people. It means, as Lisa Rhody explores in a blog post on the applicability of improvisational comedy's "rule of agreement" to academic life, adopting a mode of exchange that begins with *yes* rather than *no:* as she describes it, among colleagues, the rule of agreement functions as "a momentary staving off of the impulse to assume that someone else's scholarship is fashioned out of ignorance or apathy or even ill will or that the conversation was initiated in bad faith. Agreement doesn't have to be about value: it's not even about accuracy or support. The Rule of Agreement is a social contract to respect the intellectual work of your peers." That *yes,* in fact, creates space in which we can recognize the possibilities presented by broadening our notion of who our "peers" might be, creating a much larger "us," not set in opposition to "them." *Yes* creates the opportunity for genuine dialogue, not only among colleagues but with many more potential colleagues, as well as with our objects of study, our predecessors, and the publics we hope to engage. *Yes* encourages us to step away from competition, from the race for professional distinction. *Yes* is the beginning of *yes, and,* through which we create the possibility of working together to build something entirely new.

This mode of generous thinking is already instantiated in many projects that focus on fostering public engagement in and through the work done within the university, including—as just one example—that of groups like Imagining America, which serves to connect academics, artists, and community organizations in ways that can elicit and support their mutual goals for change. Public projects like these are well established on many campuses around the country and in many fields across the curriculum. But one key aspect of understanding generosity as the ground from which the work of the university can and should grow is the requirement that all of us take such public projects just as seriously as the more traditional forms of scholarly work that circulate amongst ourselves. Scholars working in public history, to offer just one example, have some important stories to tell about the difficulties they have faced in getting work in that field appropriately evaluated and credited as scholarship. And a few years ago, after a talk in which a well-respected scholar discussed the broadening possibilities that should be made available for humanities PhDs to have productive and fulfilling careers outside the classroom, including in the public humanities, I overheard a senior academic say with some bemusement, "I take the point, but I don't think it works in all fields. There's long been a 'public history.' But can you imagine a 'public literary criticism'?" His interlocutor chortled bemusedly: *the very idea*. But the world has long been filled with public literary criticism, from the most well-regarded and widely disseminated book reviews through large-scale public reading projects to widespread fan production. All of these are modes of literary work that reach out to nonspecialist audiences and draw them into the kinds of interpretation and analysis that scholars profess, and we ignore that work to our great detriment. How might an increased focus on engaging with a range of broader publics in and through the literary, or the other materials of our culture, enrich not just their lives but our academic fields?

Scholars' and administrators' resistance to taking such public projects as seriously as we do the work that we circulate amongst ourselves—according them the same kinds of credit and prestige as traditional scholarly publications—speaks to one of two things: first, our anxieties (and they are very real anxieties) about deprofessionalization, about association with the amateur, to which I'll return in a bit; and second, to our continued (and I would argue profoundly misguided) division and ordering of the various categories to which academic labor is committed, with a completely distinct category called "service" all too frequently coming in a distant third behind research and teaching. That ranking among forms of work isn't universal, of course; community colleges, regional comprehensive institutions, and many small liberal arts colleges often have very different means of evaluating academic careers, means that emphasize the importance of engagement with students and other publics. The expectations that push research universities to dismiss public-facing work and to devalue service, in other words, aren't inevitable, but are a byproduct of the hierarchical, competitive drive that determines so much about the ways those institutions operate. Those expectations are painfully short-sighted, overlooking the very real possibilities that public scholarship creates for rebuilding frayed relationships between the university and the publics that it might productively engage. Grounding the university's work in a spirit of generosity might encourage us to erase some of the boundaries between the work that we do inside and the work that we do outside the academy, between "scholarly" work and public work, to consider ways that all of it might have a spirit of service as its foundation. But a proper valuation of public engagement in scholarly life will require a systemic rethinking of the role that prestige plays in the academic reward system—and this, as I'll discuss in a later chapter, is no small task. It is, however, crucial to a renewed understanding of the relationship between the university and the public good.

Similarly, grounding our work in generous thinking might not only encourage us to adopt a position of greater openness to dialogue with our communities and foster projects that are more publicly engaged, but it might also lead us to place a greater emphasis on—and to attribute a greater value to—collaboration in academic life, and to understand how to properly credit all our collaborators. It might encourage us to support and value various means of working in the open, of sharing our writing at more and earlier stages in the process of its development, and of making the results of our research more readily accessible to and usable by more readers. These are all ways of working that we learned in early stages of our educations, but that, as Danica Savonick reminds me, we too often unlearn in the process of our professionalization. That professionalization doesn't involve simply deepening our knowledge of our subjects, but also learning to hide the imperfections of our early work, learning to claim our polished, finished products as our own. In so doing, we wind up closing out those who might like to be in dialogue with us, as well as those—like our own students—who could benefit from learning about our processes. Generous, generative modes of critical thinking might invite nonexperts into our discussions as they develop, bringing them along in the process of discovery.

But I want to acknowledge that adopting a mode of generous thinking is a task that is simultaneously extremely difficult and easily dismissible. We are accustomed to finding "smart" ways of thinking that rebut, that question, that complicate. The kinds of listening and openness for which I am here advocating may well be taken as acceding to a form of cultural naïveté at best, or worse, as a politically regressive knuckling-under to the pressures of contemporary ideologies and institutions. This is the sense in which Felski suggests that scholars have internalized "the assumption that whatever is *not* critical must therefore be *un*critical" (*Limits* 9). Felski posits that the critical is not a project but instead a mood, a mode of self-performance, an affect—and one to which we have limited ourselves at great cost. I would reorient this argument to focus not on the critical as the dominant mood of our work but instead the competitive, the costs of which are astronomical, not only to each individual scholar in setting a course toward stress-related burnout, but to scholars collectively in undermining our ability to understand ourselves as a community, one capable of disagreeing profoundly and yet still coming together in solidarity to argue for our collective interests. What might become possible for each of us, for all of us, if we were to retain the social commitment that motivates our critical work while stepping off the field of competition, opening ourselves and our work to its many potential connections and conversations?

Such an opening would require us to place ourselves in a new relationship to our objects of study and their many audiences; we would need to be prepared to listen to what they have to tell us, to ask questions that are designed to elicit more about their interests than about ours. That is to say, we would need to open ourselves to the possibility that our ideas might turn out to be wrong. This, it may not surprise you to hear, is an alarming possibility not just for most scholars but for most human beings to countenance, as Kathryn Schulz has explored, and it's a possibility that we will go to extraordinary lengths to avoid facing. But given the ways in which arguments in our fields proceed, and given what Schulz has called the "Pessimistic Meta-Induction from the History of Everything," it is all but certain that at some future moment our own blind spots, biases, and points of general ignorance will have been uncovered. Refusing to countenance the possibility of this wrongness makes it all the more inevitable, but perhaps keeping it in view might open us to some new opportunities. Possibly being wrong, after all, is part and parcel of what Alan Jacobs calls the "tragic risk" of thinking (*How* 36), but it's also what opens the path toward being "more aware," and toward acting "more responsibly" (49). If everything we write today already bears within it a future anterior in which it will have been demonstrated to be wrong-headed, we have the potential for a genuine exploration of a new path, one along which we develop not just a form of critical audacity but also a kind of critical humility.

Critical humility is one key to generous thinking. In the early days of working on this project, I gave an invited talk in which I tested out some of its core ideas. In the question-and-answer period that followed, one commenter pointed out what he saw as a canny move on my part in talking about generosity: no one wanted to be seen as an ungenerous jerk in disagreeing with me. It was a funny moment, but it gave me real pause; I did not at all intend to use generosity as a shield with which to fend off the possibility of critique. Generosity, in fact, requires remaining open to criticism, not least because, as Alan Jacobs pointed out in the open discussion of this book's draft, "Someone who pays close enough attention to show me where I've gone wrong is being generous to me" (Untitled comment). The importance of remaining open to criticism, of acknowledging the generosity in criticism, was powerfully illustrated for me in a series of tweets from April Hathcock, a scholarly communications librarian and lawyer who was recently engaged in establishing a new working group in her field. As the members of that working group laid out their expectations and norms for one another, one member offered "assume positive intent": be generous, in other words, in interpreting the behavior and words of others. Hathcock insisted that this expectation be accompanied by another: "own negative effects." That is to say, we must not only refrain from assuming that everyone else is in the wrong, but we also must remain open to the very real possibility that *we might be*. "Assume positive intent; own negative effects": this is generosity accompanied by critical humility, a mode that creates space for genuinely listening to the ideas and experiences of others, even when they contradict or critique our own.

Humility is in short supply across public discourse today, as noted by the project Humility and Conviction in Public Life in describing its mission, which seeks to help all of us "balance our most deeply held convictions with humility and open-mindedness in order to repair public discourse" ("Mission"). It's not, in other words, just an academic problem, but then it's probably unnecessary to point out that critical humility is neither selected for nor encouraged in the academy, and it is certainly not cultivated in graduate school. Quite the opposite, at least in my experience: everything in the environment of the seminar room makes flirting with being wrong unthinkable. And the only way to ensure one's own fundamental rightness seems to be to demonstrate the flaws in all the alternatives. This is the method in which my grad students were trained, a mode of reading that encourages a leap from encountering an idea to countering it, without taking the time in between to really explore it. It's that exploration that a real critical humility—stepping outside competition and into generosity—can open up: the space and time to discover what we might learn if we are allowed to let go, just a tiny bit, of our investment in being right.

The possibility of being wrong is not the only area of discomfort that foregrounding generosity in our thinking might expose us to, however. Felski argues of literary studies that moving beyond the limits of critique might allow scholars to be more open to the affective, to the embodied experience of the emotions. There is something to be gleaned here for many academic fields, insofar as this aspect of relating to our work as scholars is underexplored. We value objectivity and critical distance, even as we acknowledge these positions to be largely fictional. It's possible that the more we are able to free ourselves to experience and express all of the moods that underwrite our work—including curiosity, appreciation, and perhaps even difficult moments of empathy and love—the richer the work will become. But what I am hoping for in asking us to step away not from the critical, necessarily, but instead from the competitive—from the critique that is offered not in a spirit of generosity but instead as an attempt to create individual distinction—is that we might look for new ways of relating not just to ourselves and our work but to one another, and to the range of publics that we want to cultivate for the university. In turning away from the competitive, we can begin to embrace the full potential of the collaborative; in rejecting the cultivation of prestige, we can adopt a more inviting, open posture. We might be able to fully shed the adopted position of the neutral, impartial, critical observer and instead become participants in the work around us and in the communities undertaking the work. This might mean being able to more readily and wholeheartedly profess the love we feel for our subject matter without fear of sounding naïve or hokey, but it might also mean opening ourselves to more communal experiences of other emotions as well, some of them our emotions, and some of them directed at us: anxiety, fear, anger. Genuine generosity, as I'll explore, is not a feel-good emotion, but an often painful, failure-filled process related to what Dominick LaCapra has called "empathic unsettlement," in which we are continually called not just to feel for others but to simultaneously acknowledge their irreconcilable otherness. Empathic unsettlement asks us to open ourselves to difference as fully as possible without trying to tamp it down into bland "understanding." This kind of ethical engagement with one another, with our fields, and most importantly with the publics around us can be a hallmark of the university, if we open ourselves and our institutions to the opportunities that genuinely being in community might create.

It's important, however, to note our own anxieties about such a shift, not least our concerns about losing whatever tenuous hold on expertise that contemporary American culture still allows. Scholars work, from graduate school forward, to develop a professional identity based on the cultivation and creation of expert knowledge; we gather recognition for that expertise by performing it for one another, and that recognition allows us to collect the resources we need in order to do the research that shapes our careers and our fields. What risks might we encounter if we open our work to the scrutiny, or even the participation, of nonexperts? We have good cause to fear the decline of esteem for expert knowledge: as Tom Nichols argues in *The Death of Expertise*, early twenty-first century American culture does not have "a healthy skepticism about experts; instead, we actively resent them, with many people assuming that experts are wrong simply by virtue of being experts" (xiii). The effects of such active resentment within the current higher education climate include a rapid trend toward deprofessionalization of scholars and their fields, and here again, the humanities provide an ominous bellwether. In early

2016, to take just one example, the governor of Kentucky rolled out a state budget that included significant cuts for higher education in the state, but announced that those cuts would be differentially distributed. According to the governor, "There will be more incentives to electrical engineers than to French literature majors. . . . All the people in the world that want to study French literature can do so, they are just not going to be subsidized by the taxpayer" (Beam). If you love French literature that much, in other words, you're welcome to spend your life studying it, but your failure to contribute to economic growth renders you unworthy of support. Deidre Lynch has explored a variant of this danger at the heart of literary studies; understanding literature as a subject that one is compelled to study out of love—and for which one must express love—risks turning the scholar into an amateur in the literal sense of the word: a person so devoted to a practice that they ought to be willing to do it for free. Michael Bérubé's 2013 presidential address to the Modern Language Association similarly explored the extent to which the love of what we do as faculty, and our claims of willingness to work "for the love of it," have been made to serve as an alibi for the exploitation of the graduate students and adjunct instructors trying to work their way into the profession. This is, as Fobazi Ettarh powerfully argues, one of the dangers of what she terms "vocational awe," which she notes "is easily weaponized against the worker, allowing anyone to deploy a vocational purity test in which the worker can be accused of not being devout or passionate enough to serve without complaint." Feeling called to a way of life, and particularly to a way of life in service to the public good, one relinquishes one's claims to fair treatment.

But what if—and the flurry that follows should be taken as a series of genuinely open rather than rhetorical questions—what if the university's values and commitments made it possible for those of us who work on campus to develop a new understanding of how expertise is structured and how it functions, an understanding focused just a bit less on individual achievement, on invidious distinction? What if the expertise that the university cultivated were at its root connected to building forms of collectivity, solidarity, and community both on campus and off? What if the communities around the campus were invited to be part of these processes? How might we work together to break down the us-and-them divide between campus and public and instead create a richer, more complex sense of the connections among all of us? If those of us on campus were free to focus on intellectual leadership not as an exercise in forwarding our own individual ideas but rather as a mode of supporting the development of our multiple communities, could we create a richer sense of the future for our fields, and for our institutions? What kinds of public support for institutions of higher education might we be able to generate if we were to argue that community-oriented projects exist in consonance with the work that scholars do in the classroom, or in professional forms of writing, and that institutions must therefore value participation in such projects appropriately? Can we argue persuasively on behalf of using scholarly work to cultivate community, of understanding ourselves in service to that community, while refusing to allow our administrations, our institutions, and our governments to lose sight of the fact that such service is a form of labor that is crucial to the future that we all share? What new purposes for the university might we imagine if we understand its role to be not inculcating state citizens, nor training corporate citizens, but instead facilitating the development of diverse, open communities—both on their campuses and across their borders—

encouraged to think together, to be involved in the ongoing project of how we understand and shape our world?

All of these possibilities that we open up—engaging perspectives other than our own, valuing the productions and manifestations of our multifarious culture, encountering the other in all its irreducible otherness—are the best of what scholars and teachers can offer to the university, and the university to the world. And all of these possibilities begin with cultivating the ability to think generously, to listen—to our subject matter, to our communities, to ourselves. This is an ability desperately needed today, not just on our campuses but in the world at large. I have much more to say, obviously—there are chapters of it ahead—but this listening presence, in which I am willing to countenance without judgment or shame the possibility that I just might be wrong, is where I will hope to leave myself in the end, ready to listen to you.

1

On Generosity

They are trying to tell us. And we need to listen.
—HILLARY CLINTON, SPEECH TO AME GENERAL CONFERENCE

Attention is the rarest and purest form of generosity.
—SIMONE WEIL, LETTER TO JOË BOUSQUET

The last course I took in graduate school was a dissertation seminar designed to help us transition from the sometimes collective and often receptive ways we'd done our work as students—taking classes, listening to discussions, absorbing ideas, and reconfiguring it all into seminar papers designed for an audience of one—to the more independent and more active ways in which we were intended to go forward into the dissertation project, with its presumably larger intended readership. Throughout the semester, each of us brought our draft proposals to the table, to be read and discussed by the group, and we were also visited by a series of slightly more advanced graduate students, each of whom gave us a chapter in progress, which we discussed with them. One of those visitors was a young woman whose dissertation topic I do not remember today at all, though I remember one moment of our interaction at that seminar table with painful clarity. The chapter she'd given us made extensive use of the concept of the sublime, and something about it hadn't quite settled for me, so I asked her how she was defining the sublime in her project. She rolled her eyes—literally—and said, "For God's sake: awe and terror. It's Sublime 101, Kathleen."

I tell you this story not because its all too blatant *Mean Girls Go to Grad School* quality makes a particularly good case for the need for greater generosity in academic life (though that too). Rather, the instigating moment—in which I asked for clarification of a term whose usage I did not find obvious at all, thank you very much—is at the heart of intellectual work, and at the heart of our work ahead. The kind of inquiry that scholars and other writers undertake relies on the possibility of a shared vocabulary, which creates the conditions under which we might conduct a conversation about complex and often contentious ideas, in the hope that we might come to some kind of mutual understanding. But note that I've described the status of this shared vocabulary as a *possibility* rather than as something that actually exists; building that vocabulary is a project in and of itself, one that requires continual attention and negotiation. It's one of the places where scholars, and particularly scholars in my corner of the humanities, push back against one another. Some of that pushback is competitive posturing, of the sort that I think that graduate student assumed I was engaging in. In fact, that I'm describing it here as "pushback" rather than as a request for clarification reveals the ways that our internalized senses of competition can cause us to interpret a question like that as aggressive and to respond with shame: if I can demonstrate that you're misunderstanding or misusing a term I find crucial, I can go on to show why your project is fundamentally flawed (and, not incidentally, why my own work in the area is so much better). But sometimes a question like that is important, and in fact well-intended: I want to have this conversation with you, but I want to ensure that we're speaking the same language.

For this reason, many scholarly projects begin with the ritual of defining one's terms. I'm about to engage in that ritual, because I want to be certain that we're all beginning this project of exploring generous thinking from, if not the same place, then at least places that are reasonably in sight of one another. But I'm also doing so because I am increasingly convinced that the very act of building a shared vocabulary that can allow us to engage in real conversations both across our campuses and with the world is itself a requirement for generous thinking. Even more: it is an act of generosity in and of itself.

That's the key term that this chapter is going to try to define, of course: generosity. Generosity is admittedly a slippery concept, and particularly in the sense I intend. Is generosity best embodied in acts that we undertake, or values that we uphold? Is generosity something we feel, or something we do? In order to get at what I mean, I'm going to work my way through a series of ideas that bear something in common with the generosity I'm trying to describe but that aren't quite the same. In the process I'll begin to sketch the outlines of what I believe the notion of generosity might do for the university today and how those of us who work in academic environments might put it into practice as a key component of our interactions not just with one another but with the publics we hope to engage.

Acts

For starters, I want to separate the notion of generosity that we're working with from the simple act of giving and any apparent selflessness that it may entail. When I say that the relationship between the scholars who make up the university and the public that university serves should be characterized by generosity, I do not primarily mean to say that we should all be doing more volunteer work in our communities, or developing more service learning projects, or engaging in any other form of "giving back" that you might imagine. These are all enormously important activities, some of which I'll draw on as we proceed, and undoubtedly doing more in that vein would be better. The mode of generosity associated with philanthropy or volunteerism establishes the means through which those who have benefited from the advantages conferred by the university can pass those advantages on to many who do not have the same access. These generous acts can, in fact, enable us to create greater access and opportunity for more members of our communities. But there are some notable ways in which focusing too exclusively on this material, action-oriented approach to generosity may cause the transformations that I'm describing to fall short.

One of the reasons that locating generosity within generous acts would be insufficient in transforming the relationships between the academy and the public can be seen in the challenges experienced by those who spend their careers in philanthropic or other socially oriented fields. People who work in public service, and particularly in roles that are associated with a high degree of selflessness—think of social workers, public school teachers, nurses, clergy, as well as those who work for mission-driven nonprofit organizations—are highly susceptible to burnout. It's enough of an issue that the *Chronicle of Philanthropy* publishes an extensive toolkit on its website designed to help nonprofit employees avoid or recover from the burnout associated with their roles. In fact, as Adam Grant's work has explored, while giving is unquestionably good, and while those who are givers in the workplace—pitching in to help with extra projects, assisting colleagues who need support—tend to be highly successful, self-lessness can cause anyone's internal resources to run low. In a week-long series on the *Harvard Business Review* website, Grant and his colleague, Reb Rebele, demonstrate how a wide range of professionals who are committed to supporting their clients and colleagues run the risk of feeling overloaded and exhausted by that commitment. University faculty and staff are no different: all the work we do for our students, for our colleagues, and for our communities can leave us feeling we've got nothing left to give. And emphasizing the virtuous selflessness at the heart of service-oriented professions, as Fobazi Ettarh notes in exploring the "vocational awe" associated with librarianship, can serve as a means of disenfranchising those workers, preventing them from protesting problems in their institutions and insisting that those institutions do better.

Beyond the damage that such an emphasis on altruism as a professional virtue can do to our personal wellbeing and to our relationships with our workplaces, however, approaching generosity as a material, philanthropic act allows us to draw boundaries around our responsibilities to the communities in which our institutions are embedded. In so doing, we risk not only limiting our impact but in fact undermining the very relationships we seek to build. That is, the ability to say that we gave at the office (or in the classroom, or in the community center) turns the generosity I'm describing into something transactional, an exchange with both a defined location and a clear conclusion. As a result, we create specific contexts for our generous behavior that lie outside the center of our working lives. Nothing about that center need necessarily change: we do what we do, and then we bring the good of what we do to the world. Generosity in this model slips all too easily into a missionary project, in which we provide the understanding derived from our privileged position to the less fortunate around us. And, having done so, we can consider our obligation to the world to be fulfilled.

The question immediately arises, of course: Do we have an obligation to the world? "Obligation" as I used it in the last paragraph seems to bear much in common with noblesse oblige, a condescending assumption that we possess gifts that we must bestow upon the less fortunate around us. But noblesse oblige stems less from a real sense of obligation than from a particularly self-aggrandizing form of voluntarism, including in the academic environment: when we focus on the knowledge or resources that *we* can give *them*, not only do we deepen the divide between us, but we further entrench our own assumption that we inhabit the true center where such knowledge resides. We may feel that we have to give to those in need because of our station or privilege, but that "have to" is one we can easily walk away from; the commitment is entirely self-selected. This is not to dismiss the impact that many community service projects have; sharing the benefit of my knowledge and resources with those around me is indeed a generous act. The problem arises when that project doesn't equally transform us, when it remains a unidirectional *act*, of limited duration, one that I can conclude, returning to the rest of my life unchanged.

The obligation that I would instead like us to focus on in the context of generosity is one we cannot conclude, and of which we cannot absolve ourselves. As François Lachance pointed out in the online discussion of the draft of this text, "obligation" derives from the Latin *obligare*, "from ob- 'towards' + ligare 'to bind.'" That is the sense of obligation that I want to explore: that which binds us together, that which we cannot walk away from without doing grave damage both to ourselves and to the fabric of the whole. Acknowledging that we bear one another obligations does not mean that we don't have a *choice*, as members of voluntary communities, about whether to fulfill them, or that there isn't agency in the kinds of generosity I'm hoping to foster. But our common presence in a space, an institution, a community, obligates us to one another. We owe one another recognition as members of that community. We owe one another attention to the concerns each of us brings to that community. Thus Anthony Appiah describes "two strands that intertwine" in his notion of cosmopolitanism:

> One is the idea that we have obligations to others, obligations that stretch beyond those to whom we are related by the ties of kith and kind, or even the more formal ties of a shared citizenship. The other is that we take seriously the value not just of human life but of particular human lives, which means taking an interest in the practices and beliefs that lend them significance. (25)

These two strands, for Appiah, exist in an ongoing tension: we bear obligations that bind us together; we take seriously the differences that mean each of us must be allowed to go our own way. That individual, agential freedom does not relieve us of our shared obligations, but nor does the nature of our obligations eliminate the agency that all of us bear in our own lives.

This mode of obligation—one that cannot be discharged through discrete acts of generosity, but that instead must be lived—is at the heart of Bill Readings's *The University in Ruins*. In attempting to define a path out of the morass in which the University of Excellence has landed higher education, Readings turns repeatedly to the notion of obligation and its connection to community. His goal, he notes, is "an anti-modernist rephrasing of teaching and learning as sites of *obligation*, as loci of *ethical practices*, rather than as means for the transmission of scientific knowledge. Teaching thus becomes answerable to *the question of justice*, rather than to the criteria of truth" (154; emphasis in original). That connection among obligation, ethics, and justice leads to his commitment to dissensus—the willingness to dwell in an ongoing disagreement and dialogue rather than forcing a false and oppressive consensus—and to his conviction that "the condition of pedagogical practice is, in Blanchot's words, 'an infinite attention to the other'" (161). This infinite attention is an ethical obligation that cannot be discharged, and an obligation whose infinitude is created in no small part by our being-in-community; "the obligation of community," Readings notes, is "one to which we are answerable but to which we cannot supply an answer" (187).

If we are going to build and sustain the university *as* and *in* communities—that is, as I discussed in the introduction, not romanticized communities, but rather communities based in solidarity, communities based on nonmarket relations of care—then we need to be able to think about our obligations to one another, about our relationships to voluntary communities beyond volunteer work. We need to think about our *belonging*, in other words: what it means for us to belong not just to our communities but to one another as members of them. As Miranda Joseph's exploration of the structure of the nonprofit organization suggests, modes of "community" associated with private philanthropy have come to serve in the age of late capital as a replacement for public commitment to the common good. These organizations do a great deal of enormously important work, but they at times rely upon a problematic form of noblesse oblige with deep political and economic origins: I as a benefactor am obliged to be generous with what I have precisely because we are no longer committed to one another as members of a shared social structure. We do not belong to one another. Instead, the shift of responsibility for the public welfare toward private entities displaces our obligations to one another in favor of individual liberties.

What I am seeking in generosity as a potential ground for reestablishing that sense of belonging, and in so doing rebuilding the relationship between the university and the public good, then, is not a vast expansion in philanthropic activity, but something seemingly smaller and yet more pervasive. Rather than understanding generosity as transactional, and thus embodied in finite acts, I want to approach it as a way of being that creates infinite, unbounded, ongoing obligation. Generosity lies in part in the force of the commitments that we make to one another, but commitments that are based in an ethical obligation that endures beyond and outside individual agency. It's a commitment that we must continually make the choice to renew, but an obligation that persists regardless of our choice. This mode of generosity bears much in common with Appiah's description of cosmopolitanism: it is a way of being in the world that need not be "an exalted attainment," but that instead derives from "the simple idea that in the human community, as in national communities, we need to develop habits of coexistence: conversation in its older meaning, of living together, association" (30). Generosity, in my sense, both dwells in and grows from this conversation: a generosity of mind.

Focusing on conversation highlights the need for generosity to be continually renewed in order to function. Moreover, it points to the things we owe one another, the things we owe our colleagues, and also the things we owe those publics whom we hope to engage. Conversation imposes an obligation that cannot be easily concluded, that asks me to open myself again and again to what is taking place between us. Conversation thus demands not that we become more giving, but instead that we become more *receptive.* It requires us to participate, to be part of an exchange that is multidirectional. It disallows any tendency to declare our work concluded, or to disclaim further responsibility toward the other participants in our exchange. It asks us to inhabit a role that is not just about speaking but also about listening, taking in and considering what our conversational partners have to say, reflecting on the merits of their ideas and working toward a shared understanding that is something more than what each of us bears alone.

This mode of generous thinking is thus first and foremost a willingness to think *with* someone. Scholars frequently engage in this kind of work with close colleagues, in various ways—when we read their in-preparation manuscripts in order to help improve them, for instance—but it's an orientation to scholarly conversation that rapidly diminishes as we move outside our immediate circles and turn to the more public performance of our academic selves. In those modes of interaction we often feel ourselves required to become more critical—or more competitive—and we frequently find ourselves focusing not on the substance of what is being said to us, but on the gaps or missteps that give us openings to defend our own positions. That so many scholars do so much work on behalf of their colleagues and their students and the publics with whom they engage indicates that the problem is not that academics are fundamentally ungenerous. It's more that the structures within which we work, and the reward systems that let us know when we have succeeded, limit the locations and relationships within which we are encouraged to practice generosity.

As a result, while we may understand generosity of mind to be a key value within the profession, its actual enactment is not allowed to become habitual, not encouraged to become part of our general mode of being.

Values

What I am attempting to describe, then, is generosity as an enduring habit of mind, a conversational practice. But in suggesting as I did in the last paragraph that such generosity is a key value within the academy, I am suddenly faced with two pitfalls. On the one hand, treating generosity as a value risks reducing a practice to a platitude, something we can all happily claim to espouse and yet do very little to enact. And worse, the abstraction that occurs in treating generosity as a value muddies the concept, drawing it into close association with a host of other terms that I do not mean to invoke.

Many of these terms, these values, are good ones, and many of them are values that we share, or at least that we aspire to share. But being values, they are double-edged: they are the terms through which we represent the best of what we wish to be, but they pose as universals when they are often very distinctly local. The value of these values seems self-evident to those who share them, but they are often differentially applied, and they are too easily wielded as weapons against others. They evade clear definition, relying on know-it-when-we-see-it assumptions, without fully questioning who the "we" is or what position we must be in in order to see it the way we do. These values, however valuable, bear origins and histories and contingencies, all of which can too easily disappear behind assumed universals rather than insisting on our examination. And we must be willing to scrutinize those values, perhaps especially when we engage with those who may understand them to mean something quite different from what we expect. The challenge of shared values, after all, is precisely that they might *not* be shared, that they might result from assumptions that are far more local than we realize. (One such value, which I'll explore further in chapter 4, is that of the public good itself: that there should be such a thing feels so self-evident to many of us that it's shocking to run across others who find that very concept to be meaningless at best, if not an outright imposition on their sense of liberty.)

Perhaps we might see the problem in attempting to establish a set of shared values by looking at something like civility. In an ideal world, we might hold civility up as a kind of aspirational community standard; it would be great to inhabit a world, or even a campus, where everyone interacted with mutual kindness and respect. But in actual practice, the term "civility" takes on a disciplinary force. It has repeatedly been used as a blunt instrument with which to quiet dissent and protest where they quite legitimately arise. And in those moments we have come to see that there are vast differences in our understandings, even within the academic community, much less between that community and the surrounding public, of what civility means and how it should best be enacted. So while civility is a quality I value—I would be very happy if we were able to conduct all our discussions and disagreements in what I think of as a civil fashion—demanding that we behave according to *my* understanding of civility runs the risk of reinforcing inequities between those who already get to speak and those who are expected to sit respectfully and listen passively.

Similarly, in talking about generosity, I do not mean to invoke the range of positive values it brushes up against, values that might be imagined to make us all a bit nicer to one another, such as optimism or even hope. Personally I am a bit prone toward optimism, though that position has been sorely challenged by recent circumstances. There is perfectly good reason in today's world not to feel so rosy about things. Many aspects of our world are in fact getting demonstrably worse, and some things show little sign of being salvageable at all. And in the face of such circumstances, the need to put on a happy face is both counterproductive and insulting. Barbara Ehrenreich describes the peculiarly American requirement that we be unflaggingly optimistic as "driven by a terrible insecurity" (12), and she explores the ways our imperative toward positive thinking works to defuse and deflect critical attention to issues of inequity and social injustice. In this way optimism, like civility, can too readily shift from an aspirational value to a disciplinary standard used to cudgel the dissatisfied back into line.

Hope, perhaps? In the face of current events and forecasts, I find myself clinging to hope, and not entirely without reason. Authors including Rebecca Solnit have compellingly explored the necessary tie between hope and action: "Hope locates itself in the premises that we don't know what will happen and that in the spaciousness of uncertainty is room to act.... It's the belief that what we do matters even though how and when it may matter, who and what it may impact, are not things we can know beforehand" (19). Hope is, in Solnit's usage, not the optimistic sense that all will be fine regardless of what we do; hope cannot stand on its own as a form of wishful thinking. Similarly, for Krista Tippett, hope is "a choice that becomes a practice that becomes spiritual muscle memory. It's a renewable resource for moving through life as it is, not as we wish it to be" (251). Hope is in this sense not blind, not passive, but is instead linked to action and is in fact that which compels the action.

But other activist authors, and in particular several authors writing about the black experience in America, have explicitly disavowed hope. Ta-Nehisi Coates, for example, has described hope as "specious," and has written powerfully about his inability to comfort his distraught son by telling him that everything "would be okay." Rather than attempting to give him hope, he tells him instead "that this is your country, that this is your world, that this is your body, and you must find some way to live within the all of it" (13–14). Hope, for Coates, denies "the all of it," by seeking instead some better world that for too many does not, and will not, exist. This disavowal of hope does not mean that there are no joys and freedoms in the world for Coates; it is, rather, that those joys and freedoms must be found in the world as it is, rather than through a kind of hope that the dominated are often called upon to perform for others rather than being able to genuinely embody. Tressie McMillan Cottom has likewise argued that hope is an alibi too often used to disclaim the reality not just of the continuing marginalization and oppression produced by structural racism but of the ways they are reinforced, rather than dismantled, by some modes of activism. McMillan Cottom points to a "nomenclature problem" at the heart of the disagreement: "When white allies want us to be hopeful what they really mean is that they require absolution in exchange for their sympathies. And, when black people say that they are plenty hopeful we tend to mean that our hope is tempered by a deep awareness of how thin is the veneer of white civility" ("Finding Hope"). Hopelessness, for both Coates and McMillan Cottom, is not an act of giving up, but instead a deeper resistance, a recognition of and insistence upon the world as it is—a knowledge that the world has long persisted in not changing and indeed may never change, but that you have to make your way in it anyhow.

These two positions on hope are not reconcilable, and yet they not only can but must coexist and speak to one another, dwelling in the kind of dissensus sought by Bill Readings. On the one hand, for Solnit and Tippett, hope is necessary to begin the process of engagement, to inspire action; hope is the grounds, for those taking up the political, for belief that such action might have an effect. On the other hand, for Coates and McMillan Cottom, those who have been born and raised into opposition rather than coming to it as a choice have little reason to expect change, and so must rely on something other than hope as the source of an ongoing commitment not just to resist but to persist, to thrive. Where for Solnit hope is "the story of uncertainty, of coming to terms with the risk involved in not knowing what comes next, which is more demanding than despair and, in a way, more frightening. And immeasurably more rewarding" (40), for McMillan Cottom there is no not-knowing what comes next. What comes next is what has always come next, if in slightly different forms. Hope in this landscape—and in particular hope's fragility—becomes a potential distraction from the work required. In that sense hope, the belief that something new could happen, is born of privilege.

I present this disagreement not to suggest that those of us inclined to hope should abandon it; in fact, I tend to believe that those who have the privilege of hope should use it toward the good in whatever way we can. But generosity might have less to do with the particulars of whether we are able to be hopeful or whether we are able to persist even in the absence of hope than in the ability to continue thinking together despite our differences. Generosity, like Appiah's cosmopolitanism, is as much connected to the mutual recognition and honoring of those differences, perhaps especially when they cannot be resolved, as it is to our continuing determination to be in community together.

That people who in many ways inhabit the same universe—the progressive public intellectual landscape of the early twenty-first-century United States—nonetheless experience that universe with radical differences, points to the difficulty, if not the impossibility, of arriving at a set of shared values. But that is not to embrace despair or to endorse giving up in the face of it. Junot Díaz points to Jonathan Lear's concept of "radical hope," the will to continue working toward a future that seems unimaginable, arguing that it may provide "our best weapon against despair, even when despair seems justifiable; it makes the survival of the end of your world possible." Ezekiel Kweku, from a slightly different perspective, focuses on the possibilities that lie just beyond despair:

> There is no shame in arriving at despair. It's human nature. But you must keep going and find the place beyond it. And when you reach that place, you fight not because you are guaranteed to win, or even have a chance of winning. In fact, losing might be inevitable. You continue to fight, even in the face of the inevitability of defeat, because it is right and it is good. The place beyond despair is not hope, exactly, but it is a place from which you may draw nearly unlimited will, because you are no longer afraid of losing.

Whether we individually embrace hope as a compelling force toward positive political action or reject it as a performance that distracts us from the real ground on which endurance and resistance can be built is less a matter of education or priorities or a correctness of perspective—the kinds of things one can be argued into—than it is a matter of something much more basic: who we are, where we have been, what we have experienced. Recognizing that all of these most fundamental differences create deep chal-

lenges in establishing a set of shared values is the necessary beginning, however paradoxically, of the process of establishing that set
of values. That process will likely never be successfully completed.
But only by generously attending to the ways that others define
and describe the world and asking how we might be called upon
to shift our own perspectives can we begin to establish the ground
for continuing our conversation. That is to say, in developing a
practice of generous thinking, we are called upon—as I have been
in this chapter, and as scholars always are in their own projects—to
begin by working toward the possibility of a shared vocabulary.

Feelings

Working toward a shared vocabulary is a process that, perhaps
needless to say, will inevitably be fraught with misunderstanding.
Lisbeth Lipari has argued, however, that misunderstanding functions not solely as an unavoidable barrier to communication but
also as a crucial, and even productive, reason for it:

> Misunderstanding reminds us, again and again, that our conver-
> sational partners are truly "other" than us; that each of us lives at
> the center of our own world; that we each arrive independently
> "on the scene" of communication with different histories, tradi-
> tions, experiences, and perspectives; that the self is not the world;
> that perfection is impossible; and that, although human language
> is infinitely generative, there are important aspects of human ex-
> istence that are, simply, ineffable. In short, misunderstanding
> opens the doorway to the ethical relation by inspiring (or frus-
> trating) us to listen more closely to others, to inquire more deeply
> into their differences, and to question our own already well-
> formed understandings of the world. (26–27)

Misunderstanding thus has the potential to yank us out of our literally self-centered ways of thinking and encourage new connections with the others with whom we seek to communicate. This ethical relation that Lipari describes might be seen as one based in empathy, or the desire to understand the feelings and experiences of others.

"Empathy" defined in this fashion perhaps lies a bit closer in to the sense with which I use "generosity." Empathy is generally understood as that ability to bridge the gap between self and other, as that quality of openness that enables greater insight across divides of background or experience. Empathy represents an attitude toward the world that we are encouraged to cultivate—and yet, as Leslie Jamison succinctly notes, "Empathy is always perched precariously between gift and invasion" (16). Empathy has the potential to ground a deeply ethical relationship with the world, and has as well the potential to flatten that relationship into something much more troubling.

So what's the problem with empathy? First, there are the myriad ways in which empathy has been understood—or perhaps misunderstood—as somehow just being about a replication of *feeling:* your story of loss makes me sad; voilà, empathy. Second, there is the ease with which it invites expression through an appropriation of the experiences of others: "I feel your pain." Third, there is the extent to which this kind of empathy works to reify the pain of others, to concretize and associate that pain with the whole of their existence; as Jade Davis notes, the dehumanized "they" created by our techniques of empathy "are incapable of dreams and joys of their own because they are the carriers of the pain you cannot face/acknowledge." And finally, there are the uneven ways in which the call to empathy has been distributed. On the one hand, as Davis points out, empathy is engineered into technologies within which "the disenfranchised, the marginalized, the at-risk are expected to perform their pain and discomfort for those who know only comfort"; their performances provide the opportunity for the privileged to experience empathy. On the other hand, marginalized and at-risk individuals have been all too frequently told they need to empathize with the situations faced by others, without any reciprocating attempt at understanding. This uneven distribution has led to one of the most bitter divides in the United States since the 2016 presidential election: commentators have repeatedly insisted that "urban, liberal" voters must find ways to empathize with the working-class whites whose feelings of disenfranchisement and economic anxiety led them to vote overwhelmingly for Donald Trump, at the very same time that the commentators fail to empathize with those urban, liberal voters, a group largely composed of people of color whose disenfranchisement has been all too literal and whose very physical safety in their communities has been too often in question. If empathy requires a one-sided experience of feeling for those who have put you at risk, while your own pain has been reduced to spectacle—or, for that matter, if empathy requires you to be able to get fully inside someone else's head in order to care about them as human beings—it's possible that it's the wrong ideal for us to strive toward.

Given this, although we may be shocked when someone like Paul Bloom argues against empathy, as he does in his recent book by that title, it's worth thinking some about his reasons. Bloom distinguishes, first of all, between emotional empathy, "feeling what others feel and, in particular, feeling their pain," and cognitive empathy, or "the capacity to understand what's going on in other people's heads." The latter, he notes, he couldn't be against—a point I'll return to in a moment—but the former, he believes, causes far more problems for us than it solves: empathy of feeling is "biased and parochial; it focuses you on certain people at the expense of others; and it is innumerate" (42), encouraging us to make decisions that help particular individuals in the short term but that may be statistically damaging in the long term. Although this mode of empathy may appear to be other-directed, it functions through an appeal to narcissism: How would *you* feel? It privileges feelings that we are far more likely to hold for those who most closely resemble us, exacerbating rather than helping us overcome racism. The mirroring established by emotional empathy creates the inevitability of a kind of colonization: You feel victimized? I feel victimized on your behalf! And, as Davis points out, "To be in the shoes of an Other still leaves you with your own feet," feet that can step out of the simulation at any time, unchanged by the experience.

Perhaps even more insidious is the degree to which, as Amanda Hess has noted in much political discourse that followed from the 2016 presidential election, empathy has been invoked not as a means of developing a deeper connection to others but instead as a means of figuring them out with a frankly self-interested goal in mind: "it often seems to mean understanding their pain just enough to get something out of it—to manipulate political, technological and consumerist outcomes in our own favor." This is the empathy of the algorithm, and before that, the empathy of the advertising industry: those who want to know how we feel in order to get us to do something. It's little wonder that empathy might feel a bit tainted, and that Bloom might decide that we're "better off without it" (10).

But if, as Jamison notes, empathy is always delicately balanced "between gift and invasion," there remains the gift to be reckoned with. Jamison's exploration of empathy leads her to argue that its good derives from the work that it requires of us—and that this work is never merely an act of imagination but instead a process of inquiry: "Empathy requires knowing you know nothing. Empathy means acknowledging a horizon of context that extends perpetually beyond what you can see" (16). This mode of empathy bears more in common with the cognitive empathy that Bloom declares he couldn't be against than with the emotional empathy described above, but it's something more than the bland and at times invasive assumption of "understanding" that Hess describes. As in Lipari's consideration of the ways that misunderstanding might provoke us to attend more closely to others, empathy here requires putting the self and its assumptions aside. This mode of empathy is inseparable from the curiosity stimulated by imagination, but it requires a desire to understand not just that which you do not presently know but also that which you recognize that you cannot know. That willingness—to acknowledge the ineffable difference of other people and their experiences, to recognize them despite what we cannot understand, and yet to continue to try to understand despite our inevitable failures— begins to lead us away from a form of empathy focused on the vicarious and manipulable experience of feelings, and toward an ethical process that asks much more of us, a process that is much closer to the generosity I am seeking.

Practices

Dominick LaCapra, in *History in Transit*, explores the role of the historian in writing about traumatic events, and in particular the historian's responsibility for working through, in a psychoanalytic sense, the memory of trauma. This "working through," however, is not conducted in order to put away the memory that "haunts or possesses the self or the community," but rather to allow it to "be remembered with some degree of conscious control and critical perspective that enables survival and, in the best of circumstances, ethical and political agency in the present" (56). The work of the historian in relationship to trauma requires deep empathy, but while that empathy involves, as LaCapra describes it, an affective response, it is not driven by an identification with the self or community that experienced the trauma; it does not call for feeling what the other feels, or for mirroring those feelings. In fact, it's less about feeling than about a particular kind of thought process. Empathy is for LaCapra "virtual but not vicarious," requiring the historian to "put him- or herself in the other's position without taking the other's place or becoming a substitute or surrogate for the other" (65). Empathy thus becomes a process of working through, an attempt to understand, one that the historian acknowledges will only ever be partially successful, and will never be completed. That process is filled with the inevitable misunderstandings that Lipari describes, misunderstandings that have the potential to open the door to a deeper ethical relation precisely by asking us to recognize the limits of our understanding and yet keep trying. Empathy in this sense is not something we have, not something we feel, but something we must wrestle with, and something we must continue wrestling with, with no expectation of ever fully pinning it down.

Understood in this sense, empathy becomes a practice, and one key aspect of practices is that they must be practiced. Practices are regular and routine, but they are also difficult and at moments feel doomed to failure. Exercise falls into this category for many of us; so does meditating; so, for many, does writing. And LaCapra's sense of empathy is a practice as well. The thing about practices is that we move in and out of them—we do not seek to exercise every moment of the day—but we are never fully done with them, either. We do not get to check the "exercise" box off on our to-do list for all time. They become instead part of the structure of our lives, something we return to again and again. Practices are not about perfection but about a continual, impossible attempt to perfect. They are ways of being in the world.

Practices involve action, of course, but they are distinct from acts, in that practices are sustained and sustainable. Even more, they are sustaining: they create the conditions under which they can continue. This is not to say that they are easy, of course. I try to go to the gym every day, I try to meditate every day, I try to write (more or less) every day, and yet more often than not, I still struggle to get myself out of the door, into my chair, focused. But every day that I maintain the practice it becomes that little bit easier, and more compelling, to put that effort forward again the next day.

Understanding empathy, as LaCapra does, as a practice, and considering it along with some related terms like "compassion" and "care," might enable us to begin to sketch the outlines of the notion of generosity I hope to cultivate. Empathy as a practice rather than a vicarious experience asks us to return again and again to our attempts to understand the position of the other despite the certainty that this understanding will always be flawed and partial; by sustaining this practice, we can begin to improve that understanding. Similarly, compassion—literally "suffering with," a quality of mind cultivated in several spiritual traditions—asks us to recognize that all beings suffer (including us) and to focus on opening the self enough to acknowledge that suffering, not to wallow in it, but to share the desire that we all may be free from it. And care, held as an ethical principle, asks us to remember the interconnectedness and interdependence of all people, and to make choices about where to place our energies and efforts with that concern—and particularly a concern for the most vulnerable among us—in mind.

If terms like "compassion" and "care" begin to make the generosity I seek sound distinctly gendered, that is not accidental. These principles are derived in no small part from feminist ethics and praxis as developed in psychology by Carol Gilligan and in education by Nel Noddings and carried forward into today's public intellectual landscape by scholars and practitioners including Sarah Blackwood, Lauren Klein, and Bethany Nowviskie. The generosity I propose as a foundation for a renewed relationship between the academy and the broader publics with whom we interact asks us to direct our attention to the responsibility that each of us bears toward one another, a responsibility that cannot be absolved through discrete acts but that instead requires our sustained and sustaining attention. This generosity is a shared requirement to look beyond ourselves, our labs, our departments, our campuses, and seek to understand the needs of members of our broader communities, as well as others outside our communities, and even outside our moment in time. But the ties between generosity and care also remind us that such attention may be required very, very locally as well, in our most intimate relationships, and even in our relationships with ourselves. This is how understanding generosity as a practice that is meant to be sustainable helps us avoid the burnout that can result from philanthropic or voluntaristic overload: care for others requires a simultaneous care for the self, precisely so that we can be ready to return our focus to the world around us.

Lest this mode of generosity I am describing come to seem all warm-fuzzies with little practical application to the scholarly mode of being in the world, I want to turn our attention toward a specific practice through which we might begin to exercise generosity in our work. But first, there's one crucial thing that needs to be said about generosity and our expectations for it: when a person who has been injured or marginalized asks why she should have to behave generously or empathetically toward someone who has either directly or tacitly permitted that injury or marginalization to occur, she is raising a point that deserves our attention. Remembering the ways that upholding civility as a communal value has too often led to its being used as a weapon with which to silence those with legitimate complaints, we must consider the limitations of the notion of generosity that I am describing, as well as the ways that responsibility for such generosity is and of necessity should be unevenly distributed.

In the current political and educational environment, those of us in positions of relative comfort, who are privileged enough to move through our days without having our most basic sense of belonging questioned, who are fundamentally safe, might best serve the community as a whole if we are willing to exercise our generosity, by taking responsibility for engaging with those who disagree with us—not least in order to begin finding those potential allies who actually disagree with us less than they think but feel as if their own positions haven't been genuinely heard. We need to expect, and permit, these attempts at connection to fail, and yet persist in trying. We need to practice great compassion, both for those with whom we want to connect and for ourselves in the difficult act of trying to build those connections.

Perhaps the most extraordinary example of such compassion and generosity that I've come across of late is the research project documented in Arlie Russell Hochschild's *Strangers in Their Own Land.* This investigation began with Hochschild's desire to understand the deepening political divide in the United States, a challenge that led her not to bury herself in conventional academic modes of research (though the book is filled with evidence of that kind of work, too) or to seek out the voices who understand the problem from the same perspective she does, but rather, as she describes it, to try to "scale the empathy wall," to find out what those on the other side of it think—but even more, to try to understand *why* they think that way. This required an extended and rather remarkable process of deep listening, of struggling to hear and understand what the members of the Tea Party with whom she met were trying to tell her. Throughout the book, we see her asking herself whether the ideas she's forming about her interlocutors' experiences are genuinely derived from the things she's being told, or whether they're based in her own assumptions about and interpretations of what she's being told. She spent countless hours, over the course of several years, listening to their stories and shaping them into a coherent narrative that could explain their worldview—and then, perhaps most importantly, she tested that narrative with them, asking them how well it represented their understandings of and feelings about their lives. In so doing, she may not have persuaded them to change their ways of thinking, but she earned their trust, and created the conditions under which they were willing to hear her.

What surfaces in *Strangers in Their Own Land* is not just an argument about where the ideas of the far Right have come from or how they have gained such purchase in the lives of their adherents, but more importantly an argument about the reasons our forms of cultural understanding (including many of the research methods we bring to that understanding) have failed. Her work demonstrates the possibilities created through a generous engagement with those outside the academic beltway, and the damage that the failure to engage can create. Hochschild's research highlights the degree to which progressive intellectuals believe they know what's best for those on the Right—evidenced in the "What's the matter with Kansas?" syndrome—and fail to see how their arguments leave their subjects feeling belittled, demeaned, and misunderstood. It should come as little surprise that those on the Right react to such arguments about their experiences by reflexively rejecting everything that the Left might have to offer. The results of Hochschild's work—both the heartbreaking portraits she presents of people who have come to feel abandoned and disenfranchised, portraits presented without shrinking from or ignoring some of the aspects of their beliefs that we might find appalling, and the evident trust that she builds with them—reveal a rather extraordinary generosity of mind on her part. That generosity, however, is grounded in a deceptively simple practice: listening.

Listening

The importance of listening as an aspect of communicating with others has long been downplayed in Western culture; as Lisbeth Lipari notes, listening plays a somewhat sad second fiddle to speaking for most of us. In fact we too frequently treat listening as "a means of preparing one's next move" in our verbal engagements, a technique that serves "the aim of conquest and control" (15). More often than not, we listen to others' arguments in order to master them, or, even better, to figure out the best means of defusing them, of demonstrating the superiority of our own. Many of us live today in a profound imbalance between listening and talking—and worse, at least in the contemporary United States, yelling. And even when we're not the ones doing the yelling, the yelling makes it impossible to listen. We tune others out in no small part because we feel bombarded. We are losing the signal in the nonstop, 24/7, top-volume noise. It's little wonder that many of us seem to have stopped listening altogether.

That Hochschild's methodology involved hours of listening to the stories being told to her without judgment was crucial to her ability to connect with and understand the culture she was studying. That listening, moreover, had to be active: not only did she need to take in the experiences being shared with her, but she also needed to ask the right questions in order to elicit further thinking about those experiences, and she needed to frame the deeper narrative underpinning those stories in a way that her interlocutors could hear and agree with. Through this active practice, she was able to demonstrate to the people whose lives she studied that they had really been heard.

Hochschild is, of course, a sociologist; people and their cultures form her area of study, which makes the need for this mode of interpersonal engagement obvious. But connection with others that is grounded in listening may lie at the heart of what's required of all of us in order to ensure the future of all of our fields, including the humanities, the liberal arts more broadly, and in fact the university as we have known it. Anthony Appiah, in his 2017 presidential address at the Modern Language Association annual convention, points out the importance of conversation in the work that scholars and teachers do, and in particular the need to think seriously about "how to talk across boundaries—how to make ourselves heard by those who don't know why they should listen." And yet, if we what we seek to engage in is a genuine conversation, we have to ensure that we are listening as well, even if we don't know why we should, either. If we do, we might find that what we hear is not that those others don't know why they should listen, but rather that they, like us, have reasons for having decided they should not. The first step toward getting past those reasons may be hearing them out. (There are exceptions to this, however, to which I'll return in a minute.)

In order to hear out the disagreements around us, we need to understand more fully what it is to listen, even—or perhaps especially—to those with whom we will *never* agree. Lipari notes that while "listen" and "hear" appear to us to be synonyms, they in fact describe very "different ways of being in the world. Etymologically, 'listening' comes from a root that emphasizes attention and giving to others, while 'hearing' comes from a root that emphasizes perception and receiving from others" (99). Listening, then, is not just an act of taking-in, but a practice of generously giving one's focus to another. Jean-Luc Nancy similarly draws a distinction between the "simple" (or perhaps passive) state of the senses in hearing, and the "tense, attentive, or anxious state" of the senses in listening (5). Similarly, composer Pauline Oliveros, in writing about her practice of "Deep Listening," notes the ways she differentiates between hearing and listening: "To hear is the physical means that enables perception. To listen is to give attention to what is perceived both acoustically and psychologically" (xxii). Hearing, in this sense, is something that happens to the ear; listening, by contrast, is a cognitive act in which one must participate. So while it no doubt feels like we're hearing one another all the time, the question of whether we're really listening remains open.

Nancy, in fact, describes the philosopher—and perhaps, by extension, the scholar in general—as "someone who always hears (and who hears everything), but who cannot listen, or who, more precisely, neutralizes listening within himself, so that he can philosophize" (1). Oliveros likewise notes that her Deep Listening practice derived from her recognition that "many musicians were not listening to what they were performing. . . . The musician was of course hearing but listening all over or attention to the space/ time continuum was not happening" (xvii). The desire that all of us bear to leap from what we hear to our sense of what we hear, or to our own performance, rather than lingering in the at times quite uncomfortable stillness required for listening, has the effect of foreclosing engagement rather than opening it up. So when we say to someone, by way of response to a complaint or a point with which we disagree, "I hear you," we may not intend to dismiss them, but we are certainly declaring the transaction complete: "I am done hearing you, as I fully understand your point." By contrast, "I am listening" is a statement that may be too steeped in therapeutic platitudes for us ever really to voice it; as Nancy says, it "belongs to a register of philanthropic oversensitivity, where condescension resounds alongside good intentions" (4). And yet, reminding ourselves that we are listening (rather than piously informing others of that state) forms an invitation to re-main open, to adopt a position of receptivity that may lead to an unexpected connection. To listen is to be ready for that which one has not yet heard—and, in fact, for that which one might not yet be willing or able to hear.

This act of listening has everything to do with paying atten-tion, and yet attention itself is a misunderstood notion. Oliveros argues that there are two forms of attention, the focal, which acts "like a lens," producing "clear detail limited to the object of atten-tion," and the global, which is "diffuse and continually expanding" to take in the world (13). Her practice encourages the careful development of both forms, as well as the purposeful shift from one to the other. However, while this mode of attention is some-thing that one who practices learns to conduct, it is not an act of control or effort. In fact, as Simone Weil explores, the attempt to pay attention as an act of will undermines actual attentiveness: "If one says to one's pupils: 'Now you must pay attention,' one sees them contracting their brows, holding their breath, stiffening their muscles. If after two minutes they are asked what they have been paying attention to, they cannot reply. They have not been paying attention. They have been contracting their muscles" (*Waiting*, 60). On the contrary, true attention "consists of suspending our thought, leaving it detached, empty and ready to be penetrated by the object" (*Waiting*, 62). Attention requires letting go of the self, relinquishing will, and finding instead a position of radical receptivity that creates the ground for learning, for connection.

None of this is easy. Like all such practices, listening requires practice, as well as a commitment not to let our lapses convince us to stop trying. As Krista Tippett has noted,

> Listening is an everyday social art, but it's an art we have neglected and must learn anew. Listening is more than being quiet while the other person speaks until you can say what you have to say. I like the language Rachel Naomi Remen uses with young doctors to describe what they should practice: "generous listening." Generous listening is powered by curiosity, a virtue we can invite and nurture in ourselves to render it instinctive. It involves a kind of vulnerability—a willingness to be surprised, to let go of assumptions and take in ambiguity. The listener wants to understand the humanity behind the words of the other, and patiently summons one's own best self and one's own best words and questions. (40)

This, as you might guess, is where I have been leading us: listening is at the heart of the generosity I hope to inspire in the relationship between the university and the broader publics with which it interacts and on which it relies; generous listening is the necessary ground for generous thinking.

However—and this is crucial—listening as a ground for generosity, as a means of working through disagreement, must be mutual, or at least have the potential for mutuality. In recent years, and with increased frequency and intensity since the 2016 US presidential election, the press has been filled with claims that free speech is being suppressed on college and university campuses, as students and faculty protest speakers whose positions they oppose, and as administrations debate whether (if they are permitted by law) to refuse visits from figures known to espouse particularly hateful ideologies. The political Right has used these incidents to claim that they are being "silenced" on campus, suggesting that my clearly progressive-leaning embrace of listening could well be grounded in hypocrisy: we'll listen, and we'll even listen to some things that are difficult to hear, but we won't listen to *you*. What I want to be clear about is this: college and university campuses, and the communities that inhabit them, should not be required to provide platforms for those whose expressed ideologies endanger individual members of those communities or the collectives they form. We are obliged to listen, both to one another and to others, to those with whom we affiliate and to those with whom we disagree, but that obligation must be mutual. We bear no requirement to host those who have no intent of using their ability to speak as an opportunity to listen, but who in fact intend their speech as a weapon. Moreover, Krista Tippett's reference, above, to the vulnerability that listening requires of us means something fairly specific: an intellectual vulnerability more than an emotional one, and absolutely not a physical one. No one should be forced to listen to those who would brutalize them. Listening to those with whom we disagree is always difficult, and it's a difficulty with which we should be willing to wrestle, but there is a threshold between the difficult and the dangerous of which we must remain aware. Giving our attention to those who would delegitimize us can help them in doing so—and yet, if we do not genuinely listen to positions opposed to ours, we may find ourselves with fewer resources available to counter them in productive ways.

During the period when the draft of this book was open for public discussion, I visited a small liberal arts college where I was told the story of a debate held on campus in the mid-1990s between members of the faculty and a well-known if very often dismissed neoconservative policy maker and columnist, focusing on the proposal to defund the National Endowment for the Arts and the National Endowment for the Humanities. As the story goes, the columnist utterly wiped the floor with the faculty, mortifyingly so, in large part because he knew their arguments intimately—he had read them—but they did not *really* know his. They knew the ways his arguments had been described to and characterized for them by those with whom they agreed, but they had not sought out the actual basis for his reasoning, and so he was able to treat their rebuttals like the straw men they were. The problem, as Alan Jacobs might describe it, is that the faculty had long since entered "Refutation Mode," a mode in which "there is no listening. Moreover, when there is no listening there is no *thinking*" (*How*, 18). Jacobs argues that thinking requires us to confront and resist both "the pull of the ingroup and disgust for the outgroup" (23), a process that must begin with a willingness to listen.

We need, again, to be clear about the limitations of listening as a ground for generosity, and in particular about the different levels of responsibility that we bear for it. And we need to acknowledge to ourselves and to one another that none of this is easy. But it's important for those of us who are disproportionately represented within the contemporary university and who operate with the protections of various kinds of privilege and power at our disposal—racial, gendered, economic, educational—to be willing to set our comfort aside and try to listen to what those with different experiences of and positions in the world might want to tell us. It's important to keep ourselves open to the things that we don't yet know we need to hear. Listening is, in this sense, a profoundly important form of interacting with the world by paying attention to it. It does not imply agreement, merely a willingness to consider. And like the work of building a shared vocabulary that I've tried to engage in across this chapter, listening is of course only the first step in creating the space for a greater mutual engagement and understanding. But perhaps if we can find ways to model listening, to convey that we are listening, at least some others around us might be inspired to stop yelling and just talk again.

But genuine listening is sufficiently difficult, and thus sufficiently unusual, that we often do not know what to make of it when we come across it. It can look like passivity, compromise, appeasement. We might see this in Ezra Klein's exploration, published during the 2016 campaign, of what he referred to as "the Gap" in understanding Hillary Clinton, the difference between the ways she was popularly represented and the ways she was described by those who knew her best. He asked them—both allies and opponents—"What is true about the Hillary Clinton you've worked with that doesn't come through on the campaign trail?" And the repeated answer: "Hillary Clinton, they said over and over again, listens." Listening, it becomes clear, is such a radically unexpected mode of political behavior, so outside the norm, that it looks to many—even to a reporter who wants to find it praiseworthy—like a flaw. Klein acknowledges the deeply in-grained gender dynamics at work in such misinterpretations, and the reasons why our political processes today are often unkind to listeners:

> Talking is a way of changing your status: If you make a great point, or set the terms of the discussion, you win the conversation. Listening, on the other hand, is a way of establishing rap-port, of bringing people closer together; showing you've heard what's been said so far may not win you the conversation, but it does win you allies.

This was Hillary's own refrain in her address to the AME General Conference, delivered in the wake of yet another African American man being killed in a police shooting, pointing to the importance of paying attention to the families and the communities calling for criminal justice reform: "They're trying to tell us. And we need to listen."

Many of us, and for many good reasons, distrust this stated desire to listen. Listening can, after all, be performed for most ungenerous purposes. And I am undoubtedly guilty of looking back on the *what could have been* of the 2016 presidential election with an all-too-starry view. But if that election was in any sense a contest between listening and yelling—between generous thinking and its dark opposite—it's all too evident which side won the conversation. However, it's also clear from the massive marches and protests that ensued that a huge percentage of the American public has not given up on a more generous mode of engagement, and has not given up on its desire to be heard.

As a community, the university, those who work within it, and those who care about it have an obligation to work toward that more generous, more ethical mode of engagement, and that work must begin with listening, with attention. Bill Readings argued in *The University in Ruins* that listening is the primary obligation of the ethical community to which higher education must aspire: "The other speaks, and we owe the other respect. To be hailed as an addressee is to be commanded to listen, and the ethical nature of this relation cannot be justified. We have to listen, without knowing why, before we know what it is that we are to listen to" (162). Whatever it may be that, as Hillary notes, they're trying to tell us, we need to seek ways to listen. In so doing, our work as teachers, as scholars, and as members of the university community can help create the possibility for renewed relationships with the public—relationships that we desperately need today if we are going to be able to keep doing our work tomorrow.

In the chapters that follow, I'll explore different aspects of that work and how we might be more generous within it, inviting those usually outside our circles into our conversations and listening to their interests and concerns. This mode of generous thinking might begin with the very foundation of our work—reading—if we begin by understanding our engagements with the texts we read and with the other readers we encounter along the way as part of an ongoing, shared conversation, a conversation that has the potential to shape our collective experiences of the world.

2

Reading Together

If you are listening to what people are saying . . . they will explain how and why they are deeply attached, moved, affected by the works of art that make them feel things.

—BRUNO LATOUR, *REASSEMBLING THE SOCIAL*

However much we may hope to produce specifically political effects, or to "change the world" in a specified political sense, any and every effect we have in the world must be achieved through a practice of reading.

—JOHN GUILLORY, "THE ETHICAL PRACTICE OF MODERNITY: THE EXAMPLE OF READING"

A t several key moments in drafting this chapter, I found myself stricken by a particular kind of anxiety that has dogged my writing across my career, an anxiety brought on by my sense that I had not yet read enough to be certain what it was I wanted to say. The reading that I felt myself in this instance missing is a specific mode of scholarly work, one driven by something more than curiosity, or open-ended exploration of the ideas of others. This mode of scholarly reading is instead about mastery, due diligence, and the forestalling of disagreement. It's about competition, both with what I am reading and, more importantly, with the ways that I project that my own work might be read. This is not to say that scholarly reading is solely instrumental in nature, but it does strike me that my anxieties about not having read enough, and my almost uncontrollable desire to retreat from writing in order to read more before putting fingers to a keyboard, were driven in no small part by worries about competing readings, especially from readers who have read far more and far better than I, and even more from that subset of readers whose responses to what they read often begin from a position of deep skepticism.

It's possible, of course, that these anxieties are particular to me or to my field: as a scholar trained in literary studies and working in an English department, my relationship to reading is of a pretty specific nature. Not that there is one, singular, identifying mode of reading within literary studies, or within English; far from it. Reading, however, as both the subject and the method of my field, is the object of great scrutiny, and because of that concern, the sense of never having done enough of it—or worse, the nagging sense of maybe having done it incorrectly—may well be a problem local to my corner of the campus. Honestly, though, I don't think so. I suspect that worries about the reasons and the methods through which scholars engage with the materials that they study are endemic to the academic profession as a whole, and that reading might be able to serve, in this chapter, as one representative form of that engagement. In fact, looking at the role that reading plays in processes of mastery and professionalization in English departments might have something instructive to tell us about the lives and work of today's scholars in general. Reading and its associated modes of interpretation form a component of all academic fields, whether what's being read and interpreted is the previous literature on a topic or the data that has been gathered in pursuit of a hypothesis. And the ways we read that material often become a proxy of sorts for the ways that we engage with one another, with our students, and with off-campus readers. Reading, after all, goes on far and wide outside the academy—and of course one of the goals of the university is to inspire and support more and better reading in the broader public—and yet professionalized reading practices are a key marker used by scholars to distinguish themselves and the unique results of their reading. Learning those practices is a primary point of entry into the field for students, a means of moving out of the ranks of the uninitiated and into the enlightened, and thus concerns about whether you're reading enough, or reading the right material, or reading the right way are at the heart of the process of professionalization. They're also a source of enormous tension and even resentment between "professional" and "amateur" readers. And given these anxieties and tensions, given the role that reading plays for all of us on campus and the role we'd like it to play in the culture around us, given its importance in our rites of professionalization, the act of reading—why we do it, how we do it, what we might learn from it—deserves examination. So while the chapter ahead focuses primarily on the reading of books, and at times even more particularly on the reading of literature, I intend for that reading to serve as a metonym of sorts for the ways that scholars and nonscholars alike engage with the materials under study within the university. That is, reading is meant to serve here as an exemplar of the many different modes of inquiry in which scholars engage as well as the practices through which they professionalize as scholars.

The classroom's position as a space in which professional and nonprofessional readers wrestle with these practices might begin to explain why many of my worries about reading have found ground on which to flourish. It's possible that I am again mostly exposing my own personal anxieties, rather than broadly shared and even structurally generated concerns, but again, I don't think so. The classroom as a site of professionalization, as a space in which I as instructor present myself as a model of such professional practices, at times surfaces my anxieties about how I read, how others will perceive and respond to my reading, and how my reading might influence—for better or for worse—the reading of others. I worry about being insufficiently prepared, about the enormous gaps in my knowledge that might at any moment be uncovered. Those worries are at least partially driven by imposter syndrome, of course, that lurking certainty that I'm not really qualified to be doing what I'm doing and that one day all my flaws and failings will become all too apparent. But it's also, I am grateful to have been reminded by Martin Eve in the prepublication discussion of this book, part of a healthy humility, a willingness to acknowledge that I actually *don't* know everything, and that it's part of my ongoing professional purpose to continue learning. Such learning is—so obviously it's almost embarrassing to put into words—the heart of the work that we do together on campus. And yet it only gradually dawned on me over the early years of my teaching career that perhaps the classroom isn't a space in which I'm meant to focus on exhibiting mastery, but rather one in which I can model a process of inquiry with all its questions and doubts. Perhaps teaching—and by extension in the context of this chapter, any form of reading that we undertake with others—is best imagined as a collective process, in which I might set out a course and create some interactions and provide some key points of direction, but then must step aside, allowing the readers with whom I'm working and the texts that we're exploring to lead the way. Perhaps understanding myself not as the one who has to have all the answers, but instead as the one who can ask a few key questions, might shift the emphasis in the classroom—and in all of the reading practices in which I engage—from mastery to connection.

In the case of this chapter, I nonetheless (and I suppose at this point obviously) pressed forward with drafting, despite my urge to stop and read more instead, trying as in the classroom to keep myself focused on the potential for creating new forms of connection grounded in generosity. My hope is to encourage scholars—not least, myself—to revisit and reevaluate not just our own reading practices but also the reading practices of our students, which we encounter regularly in the collective space of the classroom, and of readers outside the academy, and to think about what we might learn from them. This reconsideration and even potential embrace of ways of reading and engaging through texts that focus just a bit less on mastery and more on connection may have benefits for our work with our students, pressing us to consider the ways we instruct and develop lifelong enthusiasts as well as future professional readers and learners. But there might be benefits for our scholarly work as well, affecting both the ways we think about ourselves in relationship to the acts of reading and teaching and the ways we model our work for others who care deeply about reading but do not understand why we do it the way we do.

That puzzling obstacle in encouraging myself to write this chapter, however—the fact that even now there remain too many things related to this topic that I have yet to read (not to mention that my discussion of this chapter online led to another enormous pile of recommended readings)—leads me to wonder whether there is something in the professional relationship between reading and writing, including those anxieties about beginning to write too soon, before one has read *all the things,* that might be improved by understanding the reading process itself—or the process of inquiry as engaged in across our fields—as more dialogic, more relaxed, more pleasurable. If I felt, as a scholar, a bit less of a need to demonstrate my mastery, my competitiveness, if I were able to deal with being a little bit wrong right now, and to embrace the learning that might get done in the process, might I find my way toward a more generous mode of engaging not just with the writers that I study, or the readers I write for, but with myself in the process of this work? How might an approach to reading that begins from a position of openness, of learning, of listening, help provide a clearer recognition of the inevitably provisional nature of the sentences I set down here, enabling me to produce them with a little less fear?

Writing is, of course, part of a communications circuit that both begins and ends with reading: I read things about which I write, so that others might read and perhaps even write about them in turn. It's only in the closing of that loop, in the reading, that the significance of any given piece of writing emerges. However well I write, the meaning of what I produce will ultimately be determined though its interactions with its readers. And of course the readers of most scholarly writing are other scholars, whose social, cultural, and educational backgrounds lead them to bring a particular set of methods, expectations, and purposes to the reading process. Any academic writer works—or should work—with that audience in mind. The result, however, is that academic writing is overwhelmingly (if not always, and not intentionally) produced not just for but *about* scholars, about scholarly ways of reading. This peculiarity may be most highly visible in literary criticism; any sufficiently scholarly analysis of a novel, for instance, is not about the ways that readers-in-general read that text, but rather how *academic readers* read it. The failure of general-interest readers to engage with scholarship about the books they're reading isn't due to a lack of interest in literary criticism: the flourishing of public spaces for reading and writing about books, from literary magazines like *The Millions* to social networks like *Goodreads,* makes clear that readers want to read and write about books. The disconnect stems, rather, from the fact that scholarly analyses are not only not written for general-interest readers; they are also not about them.

With some notable exceptions, academic literary criticism does not reflect or explore the ways that mainstream readers read, or the reasons they care about the thing being analyzed. Drawing on her years-long study of book clubs and their practices, sociologist Elizabeth Long argues that members of reading groups and other mainstream readers often understand books as "equipment for living," in Kenneth Burke's famous phrase; this understanding leads them to focus on the connection between what they read and their own lives, with the result that they often find scholarly practices of literary criticism irrelevant. By contrast, as Anne Gere's study of the literacy practices of late-nineteenth- and early-twentieth-century women's clubs makes clear, the academic study of literature established its professional status in large part by creating a disdain for the pragmatic, affective, and even spiritual modes of interpretation that the common reader brought to books. So while Long's suggestion that scholars assume that "their readings can stand for everyone else's, or that there is a homology between literary quality and worthwhile reading experiences" (221) may overstate the case, Gere's analysis points to a clear reason for the divide between popular and academic modes of interpretation: the maintenance of professional status—and not just for scholars but for their field. In fact, Gere notes that "to claim a place in the academy, English had to demonstrate sufficient intellectual rigor, and, in the professorial view, women's clubs offered a cultural other against which a professionalized version of English studies could be established" (212). Scholars today write for and about scholars because they assume—and not without reason—that their peers define the limits of their audience, but they also limit that audience in order to maintain and reinforce the status of peer. I'll focus in the next chapter on the ways that scholarly work, and the audience for it, might be opened up if more of it were done in and with the public. That process, however, has to begin with a richer, more generous understanding of how and why mainstream readers connect with and interpret texts, what reading does for readers in the broadest sense.

This chapter draws more heavily on my own field, literary studies, as well as on its methods and modes of citation and analysis, than does most of the rest of this book. I also found myself drawn at moments in this chapter into a more formal, technical language than I adopt in much of the rest of the book. Resisting the pull of what gets denigratingly referred to as "jargon," but is often in fact a precise professional vocabulary, is a challenge, especially as I find myself in this chapter discussing issues that lie at the heart of my field with reference to work done by my colleagues. Given both my care for their work and my concern for their perception of my own work, it would have been all too easy to slip into an insider language. That language, however, as I'll discuss both in this chapter and at greater length in the one that follows, risks closing other interested readers out of the discussion. My hope has been to keep this argument as open and accessible as possible, to include readers of many different kinds, and of many different genres, both across and beyond the university. Reading is one of the crucial processes through which all of us—scholars, students, book club members, and casual readers—have the potential to come into a more generous relationship with the world. Through reading, we learn not only to understand ourselves but also to understand others, both in relation to and in their ineradicable difference from ourselves. And reading *together* is at the heart of how the university operates, how we both teach and learn. But that teaching and learning requires that we scholars not only share the materials of our fields and our interpretations of them with those around us, but that we more generously open ourselves to honor the ways that others read as well. It is not just in the experience of authors or characters that we can learn to appreciate difference through reading, but also in the experience of other readers reading. All of us—professional and lay readers alike—will benefit from thinking a bit more collaboratively, and a bit less competitively, about how others read, and why they read that way. And it might make us all a bit more sensitive to the possibilities and nuances embedded in reading itself, as we experience a text from multiple perspectives, understanding the multiple ways that things can be read and the potential impacts those readings can have.

If scholars hope to promote a vision of scholarly work, even at its most critical, as being rooted in and working toward the public good, we need to find ways to engage broader publics with that work. We could do worse than beginning by revisiting the practice of reading itself to seek a new understanding not solely of how scholars read, or for that matter how general-interest readers read, but *why* all of us read.

Why Do Readers Read?

Scholars and general-interest readers alike read to learn, of course, and many of us read for work, but self-identification as a *reader* stems from a prior, seemingly simpler motivation: we read for pleasure. Readers read because we like to read. So where Alberto Manguel would propose thought as the origin of the desire to read—"We read to understand, or to begin to understand" (7)—I want to suggest instead that feeling may be primary in underwriting our attachment to reading. It is the presence of that pleasure that pushes the reader onward into the text. This is the position from which Alan Jacobs begins his exploration of reading: "Forget for a moment how books should be read: Why should they be read? The first reason—the first sequentially in the story that follows but also the first in order of importance—is that reading books can be intensely pleasurable. Reading is one of the great human delights" (*Pleasures* 10). That delight is meant, more than anything, to be indulged. And thus Jacobs's guiding principle for those who wish to know what to read: *Read at Whim*.

But where exactly does the pleasure in reading lie? Does it manifest in the same ways for lay readers as it does for scholarly readers? Elizabeth Long has pointedly argued that "academics tend to repress consideration of variety in reading practices because of our assumption that everyone reads (or ought to) as we do professionally, which usually involves a cognitive or analytic approach to texts" (11). Again, Long's charge may be overstated; significant threads of literary studies beginning in the 1960s, and perhaps most famously including the work of Janice Radway, have focused on reader reception and engagement. Radway's *Reading the Romance*, in fact, enjoined the field to think about everyday readers in serious ways, and her work has inspired a

wide variety of explorations of the ways that audiences encounter and make use of texts. Whether Radway's insights have been
taken up as fully and as broadly as they might be is, however, an
open question. Given that differences in *how* we read, which seem
inevitable, are inevitably accompanied by significant differences
in *why* we read, it is worth considering how the different pleasures
that different readers find in the process might speak to one another. The long tradition of educating lay readers to become scholarly readers has likely lent us a sense of the instructive value of
the pleasures of scholarly reading, but what might scholars learn
from the pleasures of general-interest readers and the reading
they do?

Manguel describes the pleasure in reading in ways that evoke
long journeys, new discoveries, passionate love affairs: "We read
to find the end, for the story's sake. We read not to reach it, for the
sake of the reading itself. We read searchingly, like trackers, oblivi-
ous of our surroundings. We read distractedly, skipping pages. We
read contemptuously, admiringly, negligently, angrily, passionately, enviously, longingly. We read in gusts of sudden pleasure,
without knowing what brought the pleasure along" (303). We do
not read in any one consistent way, in other words, but instead are
pushed and pulled by the text and swept along by the desire for
more. That desire, and the pleasure that can result from it, often
lies in the encounter with the unexpected, the discovery of that
which we didn't quite know we were looking for. In many cases,
this exploration is bound up in what Peter Brooks described as
"reading for the plot," following the unfurling of a story with its
many conflicts and coincidences, revelations and reversals. We
read, in these cases, to find out what happens. Or, as Rita Felski
argues, we read for recognition, we read for enchantment, we read
for knowledge, we read for shock (*Uses* 14). In reading, we enter

into another universe, into other lives, and, in so doing, tempo-
rarily escape our own. We read for the ways that we are bodily
taken up by a text. Or we read for insight into our own world, for
self-discovery, for advice. We read for comfort. We read for the
deepest kinds of personal understanding.

Interestingly, the appeal to personal, emotional, affective purposes in reading has at times been experienced by scholars of literature as a disciplinary command to which they are required to
submit. Deidre Lynch's wide-ranging exploration of the eigh-
teenth- and nineteenth-century institutionalization of literature
as an object of love, for instance, contains a powerful critique of
the extent to which "those of us for whom English is a line of *work*
are also called upon to *love* literature and to ensure that others do
too" (7). Enforcing that emotional performance—particularly
given, as I discussed in the introduction, the degree to which the
twenty-first century economy consistently devalues anything we
do for love—is a means of erasing the labor involved in academic
work, and Lynch is right to resist it. But my goal in this chapter is
not to impose a requirement on scholars that we commit to love
as the prime mover in our relationships with the materials of our
fields; rather, I hope instead that all of us (professors and profes-
sees, readers ordained and lay) might simply consider the power
of a personal, emotional relationship to reading and the role that
such a relationship might play in drawing others to reading with
us, in making visible the joys of what scholars do so that it might
be more appropriately valued off-campus as well as on.

Perhaps even more dangerously, the appeal to the delight that
we took in reading as children runs the risk of nostalgia, a fond
backward-lookingness that can transform every sense that things
are different now into a sense that things are *worse*. It is perhaps
ironic (or perhaps just human) to discover, despite the work I've

done toward uncovering and debunking this narrative of decline with respect to the relationship between literature and newer media forms across my scholarly work thus far, that I am just as subject to that nostalgia as anyone. I remember being able to read for hours as a child, utterly undistractable until someone forced me to *put the book down and go outside already,* and I long to recover that feeling. What I miss most is really being able to single-task, having the attention span and the absence of competing demands necessary to focus on a book to the exclusion of all else. I'm far from alone in this yearning for what reading once was, perhaps needless to say, but that yearning is inevitably romantic in its gauzy depiction of what reading can or should be, and the longing for that more innocent time may in fact mask a bit of condescension. Thus we see Lynch's evaluation of the nostalgia she senses in graduate student complaints about the ways that the professionalized practice of literary criticism in which they are trained "smothers" the love of the material that led them to undertake the study. That nostalgia, she points out, is itself in fact a pathway to professionalization; one of the key methods by which scholars have separated themselves out as professionals is precisely by "ascribing charisma, authenticity, and a capacity for true feeling to amateurs" (351). This is a trap that I hope to avoid: when I suggest that there might be something for us to learn from the ways that general-interest readers read, I do not necessarily mean to hold those readers up for our praise or our scrutiny—not, at least, unless they are actual readers with whom we are interacting, rather than some hazy idea about readers that we have developed as a strawman for or as a potential avenue of escape from our own travails. But I do nonetheless want to consider some of our ideas about amateur readers, and in particular how we understand their experience of reading for pleasure.

For such a key motivation for textual engagement, after all, pleasure in reading has been soundly denigrated among professional readers, in which category I'd include scholars, of course, but also mainstream literary critics and, perhaps surprisingly, some parts of the library profession, in which, as Barbara Fister points out, the "provision of information (whatever that might mean) is valorized, while pleasure reading is seen as a popular but far less culturally significant function" ("Reading"). Reading for pleasure is a mode associated with the amateur, and professionals of all stripes become professionals in no small part by separating themselves from it. Saying that one "enjoyed" a book, after all, does not carry much substance. Too personal or inwardly focused an attachment to books risks association with the self-indulgent, and even the auto-erotic. Ways of reading that are too closely tied to escapism, such as reading for the plot, are waved off as passive and superficial. Ways of reading that are too focused on the interior lives of characters and the identifications they inspire are dismissed as therapeutic. As Rita Felski argues, if critics and scholars discuss the experience of enchantment in reading at all, "they are inclined to diagnose it as a displacement of real-world issues, a symptom of something else" (*Uses* 57). And the books that many readers find most pleasurable—genre fiction of many different kinds; young-adult fiction; chick lit—have too often been treated as uninteresting, insufficiently serious, and even detrimental to health and intellect. Elizabeth Long suggests that this dismissal of whole categories of reading and the pleasures that they generate is bound up in the scholarly desire to control what is understood by reading, shoring up scholarly authority by promoting the "tradition of Great Books" to the exclusion of all other readerly experiences (30). Anne Gere similarly notes the extent to which professorial anxieties about the potential feminization of their profession led them to "seiz[e] the authority to serve as arbiters of culture" (217), establishing the boundaries for cultivated literary taste. But scholars are far from alone in the desire to establish their professional credentials through such judgments; popular critics have long built their reputations—see Michiko Kakutani—as authorities through the creation of hierarchies of literary value. And, contra Long, a quick perusal of a recent Modern Language Association convention program will make clear the enormous diversity of texts and genres and media forms actually being studied in English departments today. But Long's larger point is worth considering: "May readers not find something worthwhile in even a 'bad' book?" (30). And may they in fact not find something of importance to themselves in "bad" reading practices? However much the role of professors of literary studies might include encouraging student readers to shift their attention to texts of particular historical or aesthetic significance, or to engage in particularly instructive methods of reading, this education need not include a dismissal of the ways they read on their own, even—or perhaps especially—when those ways of reading are bound up in pleasure. In dismissing pleasure, professionalized readers may lose access to something crucial to full engagement with and understanding of the role that reading plays in many lives.

And, in fact, what pleasure is replaced by when it gets pushed aside is too often anxiety: anxiety about whether we're reading the right stuff, or reading for the right reasons, or reading in the right way. Robert Scholes traces one line of these anxieties about literary reading to the rise of the New Critics, and in particular to Cleanth Brooks and Robert Penn Warren's disdain for popular verse: "What is important is that this attitude—the wholesale 'correction' of popular taste—taken up and magnified in hundreds of classrooms across the country, had the effect of purging the curriculum of the very poems that had once functioned to give students textual pleasure, thus preparing them to take an interest in poetic texts that did not display their hearts so obviously on their verbal sleeves" (16). Reading poetry, under the rule of the New Critics, became work, and often intimidating work at that, leaving too many readers convinced that they could not read and understand poetry. Which is to say that students may have a point when they complain that too many of their classes destroy the pleasure of reading for them; the easy pleasures that reading held for us as children cannot survive in an environment in which popular taste is something that demands correction.

This is of course not to say that reading is never, or should never be, work. There are important pleasures to be gained from wrestling with difficult texts and difficult ideas, and it is the role of teachers to help initiate students into those critical pleasures. As Alan Jacobs has noted, "Some forms of intellectual labor are worth the trouble," in that they make us better readers and better thinkers, and because the virtues that he suggests difficult texts can lead us to—"strength and concentration and patience and humility"—can in turn produce even "greater delights" (*Pleasures* 50). Developing the capacity and desire to engage seriously with difficult material is a core aim of higher education: building the focus and curiosity and patience necessary to work through a complex text, as well as the knowledge base and insight to delve into that text's references. But developing those skills and uncovering the greater delights to which they can lead requires careful modeling, leading students from the more accessible to the less. In so doing, it might be possible for us to seek ways of building on rather than undermining the more common experiences of readerly pleasure they already know.

Or that they once knew. Students in increasingly early stages of their educations are today taught methods of reading that put them on the defense: they are set on the watch for things they might have missed; they seek patterns, symbols, and (sigh) themes. They are encouraged to set up a perimeter between themselves and the text to be sure that nothing escapes. In the current educational environment, much of the blame can be laid at the doorstep of testing, as well as the political and economic conditions that have led to testing's dominance within our schools. Under this regime, reading is understood to be a utilitarian practice designed to extract The Answer from a text, such that it can be expressed in conformity with the rest of the class, all of whom seek to echo the instructor's or the test creators' wishes. Not only is there no room for interpretation in any rich, imaginative sense; there is no room for anything other than anxiety about the consequences of getting the answer wrong. The result, as Timothy Aubry has explored, is that the complex act of engaging with a difficult literary text and negotiating its meanings is reduced to "getting it": "'Getting it' of course analogizes the act of interpretation with the act of consumption . . . once you 'get' the book . . . your work is presumably finished, and you can relax. You have it in your possession, which means you are now among the elect and are thereby entitled to appreciate what has become your property, the book's meaning, without further struggle" (47). But more sophisticated modes of textual engagement require forms of cultural privilege from which many readers have been excluded. Ideally, the role played by scholars is to assist with the struggle that difficult texts require and to convey the pleasures to which that struggle can lead. This is, in fact, the role we try to play in the classroom. Is it possible for us to play that role with the broader reading public as well?

It is worth considering, however, the extent to which—
intentionally or not—the effect that the academy actually has on
the general reading public's relationship to textual difficulty is precisely to *create* the exclusion many readers feel. Elizabeth Long
and Anne Gere both point to the role of professionalization
within literary studies in creating barriers to entry for many mainstream readers. Long notes that the rise of "specialized technical
terms"—the at times difficult vocabulary of critical theory—has
worked to close broader audiences out of literary discourse, even
where the scholars deploying those terms possess a "genuine desire to link literature to its social and political concerns" (71). This
is precisely the kind of claim that, as I discussed in the introduction,
causes many humanities scholars to bristle, irritated at the suggestion that our fields are somehow not entitled to a specialized expert language—a suggestion that resonates all too well with the
anti-theoretical, anti-intellectual dismissal of academic work
within the culture at large. Irritated humanists might thus be
prompted to inquire whether Long's own field of sociology lays
itself fully open to the people it studies, or whether it is written
mostly for insiders. That response might, if examined closely
enough, lead us to suspect that the boundaries and defenses created by professionalized knowledge serve not just to separate the
academy from the surrounding public but also to establish authority *among* academic fields. Gere in fact notes that this conflict
manifested within the field of English studies as well; the professionalization of the field during the late nineteenth and early
twentieth centuries grew not just out of a contest between professors and lay readers, but also out of a conflict "between the critics and scholars" within departments. Gere notes that critics, who
as Gerald Graff describes them in his history of the profession of
literature studies embraced Matthew Arnold's view of culture and

the humanistic tradition, "emphasized aesthetic approaches and, accordingly, tended to blur distinctions between amateurs and professionals. Scholars, however, drew on philology, emphasized mental discipline, and sought to make English studies intellectually rigorous enough to justify its place in the academy" (212). Professionalization and its manifestations arise, in other words, out of the need to prove that literary studies is sufficiently serious to belong on campus, but the success of that justification winds up radically reducing the possibility of dialogue with readers off-campus. In the next chapter, I'll think a bit more about the ways that a reexamination of some of the more public-facing modes of work espoused by the critics might help scholars engage with broader audiences, not least by developing a greater flexibility in moving back and forth between the technical, precise vocabularies with which we address one another and more open modes of address that can help get us past the language barriers surrounding scholarly work and welcome off-campus readers into engagement with the complex texts and methods we study.

In the meantime, however, we might reflect on the reasons our critical vocabularies might be off-putting to those broader publics—not just, I suspect, because they do not understand them, but also because they understand perfectly well the insult our approaches often pose to the reading practices of the uninitiated. Eve Sedgwick argued in 2003 that one problem scholars have had in sustaining alternatives to what Paul Ricoeur labeled the "hermeneutics of suspicion" was precisely that the vocabulary deployed in describing those alternatives was often "so sappy, aestheticizing, defensive, anti-intellectual, or reactionary" that no scholars worth their salt were willing to explore much less embrace another path. Sedgwick goes on to suggest that this problem is due to "the limitations of present theoretical vocabularies" (150), and that new modes of engagement with the affective dimensions of the materials we study might become more possible with the development of better terms, including perhaps her own "reparative reading." The suggestion is that scholars resist exploring readers' use of cultural materials as "equipment for living" because the language used in discussing that relationship makes us cringe. But the key problem is not that the sappiness turns scholars away; it's that scholarly cringing in the face of perceived sappiness is visible. Developing a vocabulary that allows us to describe general-interest readers' motives as "reparative" and their engagements as "affective," as Sedgwick proposes, might grant their modes of reading a seriousness of purpose and of impact that allows us to justify their study on campus, but dismissing the terms that readers themselves use to describe the importance of reading in their lives, and worse, declaring modes of reading that emphasize emotion or identification or self-improvement to be insufficiently rigorous—see, for instance, scholarly responses to the idea of the "relatable" text—puts those readers on the defensive against us.

It's not just a matter of the terms that we use when we theorize the ways that readers read, in other words, that grants those readers seriousness of purpose. Establishing concern for general-interest readers requires a broader approach from scholars, as well as a recognition that such readers often have more sophisticated understandings of their own practices than we might assume. This insight emerges from Janice Radway's close engagements with women readers of romance novels, and it is sustained in contemporary studies of a wide range of fan cultures and other projects that do more than conduct pith-helmeted excursions into the land of lay readers, but that instead honor and try to engage with those readers *on their own terms,* seeking to understand their own interpretations and judgments. If university-based approaches to the study of readers and reading were to begin from a position of generosity, listening as readers explore their own practices instead of using scholarly terms and values to dismiss their reading practices as somehow suspect, we might be able to establish common ground between us, rather than making those readers the subject of our expert scrutiny. If the pleasure of reading—including, or perhaps even especially, reading the most mass-market novel we can imagine—lies in what it can help the reader feel, then perhaps, rather than dismissing that engagement as somehow suspect due to its lack of critical distance, we might instead take that feeling, and its description, seriously. If a text serves a therapeutic role in the lives of its readers, if a book is treated as "equipment for living," that relationship might be more complex than we assume. As Rita Felski argues, readerly experiences such as enchantment are "richer and more multi-faceted than literary theory has allowed; it does not have to be tied to a haze of romantic nostalgia or an incipient fascism" (*Uses* 76). In fact, she notes, understanding literature's meaning as emerging from the ways that it is used opens up "a vast terrain of practices, expectations, emotions, hopes, dreams, and interpretations" for new kinds of scholarly exploration (8).

That exploration might reveal that readers have compelling reasons for privileging emotion or utility or even escape in their interactions with books. Or they may not. Alberto Manguel describes two roles that readers play in their interactions with the texts they read: "that of the reader for whom the text justifies its existence in the act of reading itself, with no ulterior motive (not even entertainment, since the notion of pleasure is implied in the carrying out of the act), and that of the reader with an ulterior motive (learning, criticizing) for whom the text is a vehicle toward another function" (184). It may well be that readers want nothing more from the books they read than that they be books, enabling for the reader nothing more than the act of reading. As scholars for whom the act of reading is always inevitably motivated (the text is always either a source for writing, or an object for teaching, or, in all too rare moments, an avenue of escape), such a relationship is puzzling, to say the least. We should not, however, assume without question that such a readerly position is naïve.

Beyond Naïve Reading

This seems an opportune moment to step back to the wide-angle view I'm attempting to take in this chapter, at least in part, in which "reading" stands in for a broad range of interpretive practices that take place in the encounter with an equally broad range of kinds of texts. Most of what I'm describing here, emerging as it does from English studies, focuses on reading books, and especially on reading literature. But of course everyday readers read a wide range of other material as well: they read advertisements, they read newspapers, they read reports, they read information. And the most cursory look around the culture of the United States today will make all too clear that those readers don't always read well. So by arguing that scholars should do a bit more to understand and honor the ways that off-campus readers read, I do not mean at all to suggest that all of their readings are equally *good*—just that they equally *are*, and that those readings often do significant work in the lives of those who perform them. If the university is going to fulfill its public mission of creating more, better readers across a wide variety of fields, we need not only to think very carefully about what we mean by "better," but also to understand how and why actual readers currently read. We can't just reject those hows and whys as wrong; we have to begin with them and try to build on them to make them better. What I'm asking of scholars, then, is not simply that we indiscriminately celebrate popular reading practices but that we seek to understand the serious work those reading practices do for many people, bringing the generosity of improv's "yes, and" perspective, rather than our more habitual "well, but" to our engagements with those readers.

This is not easy, especially when we start thinking about the reading of things other than literature, as so much public discourse seems to have been taken over by a spirit of absolute rejection rather than even the reasoned "well, but" argument. As Tom Nichols has argued, contemporary culture is permeated by active resentment of experts and the determination to reject anything that smacks of expertise. This kind of rejection is visible across academic fields—the rejection of climate science, the rejection of evolutionary biology, the rejection of political theory—and so it's not a surprise, perhaps, that popular arguments about literary reading are rife with it as well. As an example, take the stance of philosopher Robert Pippin, who in a 2010 *New York Times* essay defending the more appreciative engagements of untrained readers of literature, argues that "poems and novels and paintings were not produced as objects for future academic study; there is no a priori reason to think that they could be suitable objects of 'research.' By and large they were produced for the pleasure and enlightenment of those who enjoyed them." True enough, perhaps, though by this logic one would be hard-pressed to think of *anything* presenting an a priori reason for research. But no matter: Pippin's column encourages its readers to open themselves to the possibilities and pleasures of "an appreciation and discussion not mediated by a theoretical research question recognizable as such by the modern academy," a mode that he happily labels "naïve" in its escape from disciplinarity and embrace of enjoyment.

I hope it's clear by this point that I am greatly sympathetic to—in fact, arguing on behalf of—the desire to open conversations across reading communities and to create the opportunity for participation in those discussions by readers not schooled in contemporary theoretical discourse. Like Pippin, I insist that a proper valuation of enjoyment is necessary. However, that valuation need not be accompanied by a rejection of the critical or theoretical, and certainly not a rejection of the value of research, as if it were impossible for enjoyment and critical thinking, or deep research and an experience of wonder, to exist simultaneously. Generous thinking need not, in other words, rely upon the category of naïveté in opposition to the academic. Instead, I encourage us to ask what avenues of engagement with the world and its readers might open up to us if we were instead to begin from the assumption that reading is never naïve, that there is always a wrangling with meaning underway, and that there is always something being learned. Can we ask, with Rita Felski, what it might mean "to treat experiences of engagement, wonder, or absorption not as signs of naïveté or user error but as clues to why we are drawn to art in the first place" (*Limits* 239)? How might we begin to understand the function of scholarship in dialogue with reading-in-general? And how might that understanding begin to shape a more productive relationship between the academy and the broader public?

A first step in this process could involve thinking about the kinds of work that we regularly do in our classrooms, especially in early undergraduate courses—not thinking about that work in order to change it, but rather thinking about it in order to understand how the engagements we foster in the classroom and the positions we develop and embrace as instructors might point the way to potential connections with the publics around us. Much of our effort in those scenes of reading instruction has to do with making what feels obvious instead appear strange, asking our students to step back from something that seems familiar or transparent and instead look at it obliquely. The goal in this shift of position is ideally less to get our students to think in some specific way about the object than it is to get them to recognize their own perspectives and the role those perspectives play in their appreciation of the object. In this way, they—and we—can recognize that every reading presupposes a theory, that even the most text-focused modes of close reading aren't just a careful accounting for detail but rather an argument about where a text's meaning is to be found, how it can be understood, and who is responsible for having put it there. In order to encourage this interest in perspective, however, we need to begin from rather than reject readers' immediate experiences of the text, even where they seem to us sentimental or superficial. As Timothy Aubry argues, "Emotional responses to literature are themselves complicated forms of interpretation and knowledge, fully capable of holding their own when confronted with the rigors of critical debate" (13–14). Rather than setting aside emotional responses in favor of critical distance, the more fruitful approach is to dig into such responses, to figure out how they are produced and what kinds of work they do.

Part of what I am up to here is encouraging scholars to leave behind the sense that emotional responses and critical distance are somehow opposed modes of reading, one of which must be shaken off in order for a reader to be educated into the other. We push aside the emotional in part because of its subjectivity; there is a limit to our ability to share highly personal responses to the things we read. And we wind up focusing on readings based in critical distance in part because their apparent objectivity allows them to be argued for, to serve as the basis for persuading others. In suggesting that we spend more time exploring personal, emotional responses to reading, however, I am not suggesting that we reject the critical mode. Rather, what I'd like us to question a bit further in trying to think about the emotional and the critical together is why we consider some readings of a text—usually the ones we can be persuaded by—to be "better" than others in the first place. Stephen Best and Sharon Marcus, in their call for a reevaluation of what they refer to as "surface reading," point to the overwhelming influence of Fredric Jameson's argument that, as they summarize it, "only weak, descriptive, empirical, ideologically complicit readers attend to the surface of the text." What reader could stand up to such a characterization? Very few professional readers, I'd imagine, who have since followed Jameson, consciously or not, in understanding the role of the "strong" critic as "wresting meaning from a resisting text or inserting it into a lifeless one," an inescapably masculinist relation of domination that comes to characterize the professionalism of the academic profession itself (Best and Marcus 5). While it is undoubtedly true that some interpretations might open up greater potential for understanding the object being read and its relationship to the broader culture, or that one interpretation might be more satisfying than another in some particular intellectual way, and while I will acknowledge that these understandings and satisfactions are key scholarly goals, the notion that some readings or readers are "weak" and others "strong" lays the groundwork for reading as a quest for individual distinction, in which I must undo all of the interpretations that have gone before in order to demonstrate that mine is the best: this is reading as a competitive exercise.

One model for surface reading that Best and Marcus posit is an "embrace" of the descriptive and the empirical, of working with what's there rather than questing after what's been repressed, a stance that they call both "affective and ethical": "Such an embrace involves accepting texts, deferring to them instead of mastering them or using them as objects, and refuses the depth model of truth, which dismisses surfaces as inessential and deceptive" (10). I would argue that this mode of embrace need not remain wholly affective in order to be ethical; it need not utterly defer to the text or categorically refuse interpretation as a reading practice. In fact, allowing both to coexist—finding ways to move fluidly between emotional response, descriptive attention, and the interpretive development of meaning—might be one means of undermining the competitiveness that lies at the root of professionalized reading practices. As Anne Gere points out, professionalization in literary studies arose in no small part through late-nineteenth and early-twentieth scholars' rejection not just of the practices of public readers (and especially those personal-development oriented practices engaged in by women's clubs) but also of the publicly directed modes of work done by critics; both of these groups were treated by scholars as competitors for authority over the value and meaning of texts and for standing within the culture. Similarly, in the contemporary moment, Martin Eve reads a form of competitiveness being enacted between literary scholars and literary novelists, whose fiction at times manifests "hostile reactions to practices within university English," and sees evidence of "a fascinating power game" being played out between two sets of literary professionals competing over the terrain of "cultural authority" (*Literature* 14–15). Such competitiveness is endemic to contemporary culture; it feeds the rejection of expertise as well as the dismissal of the popular, and it makes it appear that we inhabit a Manichean world of opposed choices in which we must take sides: depth *or* surface, emotion *or* critical distance, beauty *or* analysis, pleasure *or* thought, theory *or* naïveté. It's this competitiveness, I increasingly believe, that builds a wall between the scholarly and the "common" reader, one that functions much like the empathy wall that Arlie Russell Hochschild argues exists between the Right and the Left in the United States today. It divides professional and nonprofessional readers in ways that have made mutual understanding all but impossible. As a result, our students complain, however unfairly, that we want to eliminate all the pleasure from reading. And we, no less, are left baffled and even angered by the ways that mainstream readers read. The wall created by competition, in other words, has powerfully limiting effects on the ways that scholars are able to engage with nonscholarly readers both on and off campus.

Many of the differences between the ways that general-interest readers read and the ways of reading of "literary professionals," broadly construed—not just professors, but public-facing literary critics as well—may in fact stem from the role that competition plays within the different environments in which we read. Literary professionals by and large understand the effects of the texts they read, and the effects of the interpretations they produce, to have their primary impact within the realm of the literary itself, whether that realm is understood through a model of literary history, or of cultural representations, or of more generalized discourse. At times this impact extends to the broader culture and its understandings and structures, but for the most part the literary is the arena within which texts and interpretations act, and their acting is often posed as agonistic: this author's influence overshadowed the work of his successor; this critic rejected the arguments of his rival; this scholar restored the work of that author to its deserved but previously overlooked glory. Books and ideas and authors and critics fight for attention, for recognition, for esteem; they compete in a marketplace of sorts, in which one gains value at the expense of another.

By contrast, for the general reader, the world within which texts and readings interact is the life-world rather than the literary world. Books engage and enrich the reader; they do things for *people* rather than for the world of texts or the cultures they move in. Acknowledging that perspective might encourage us, in the words of Clara Claiborne Park, to consider the ways "we would teach literature if we were in fact convinced that what we were doing could make a person different" (7). And as I'll dig further into shortly, this potential applies not just to the transformation of the lives of individual readers, but to the transformation of communities: if we could think about the ways that reading affects the building and sustenance of community, we might be encouraged to step outside of the literary or scholarly marketplace of ideas, and instead to focus a bit on the more collective economies that structure much artistic and educational exchange. Lewis Hyde most famously wrestles with this tension in *The Gift*, which he begins with the argument that "works of art exist simultaneously in two 'economies,' a market economy and a gift economy. Only one of these is essential, however: a work of art can survive without the market, but where there is no gift there is no art" (11). And, I would argue, no education. Leaving not only the materials that we study but our theories and interpretations of that material caught in a battle for market share undermines the potential they may have for genuinely affecting the lives of the individuals and groups who come in contact with them.

It is entirely likely that, for many of the readers of this text, intellectual alarm bells have been set off by the instrumental and even therapeutic role that this sense of reading's effects on readers may suggest, but the fact remains that what literature can *do* is a significant portion of its appeal for many readers. And while helping those readers develop encounters with literature that draw on more sophisticated forms of understanding is undoubtedly a laudable goal, it's worth considering that the uses readers make of literature may be more complex than they initially appear. As Aubry notes in his study of the therapeutic uses of middlebrow fiction among contemporary readers, "The greatness that American readers attribute to literature generally does not preclude, but in fact depends upon their ability to find personal relevance in the books that they read," and that sense of relevance often derives from a sense of connection to and analysis of those books' characters (16–17). The meanings and pleasures that derive from an empathic response to a character's situation, that is to say, draw on often complex processes of interpreting both personal experience and textual representations and of establishing connections between them. So identification—"mere identification," as we too often refer to it—is far from simplistic. As Rita Felski points out, identification can develop through a complex combination of alignment, allegiance, and affinity; identification might be automatic, or it might be strategic (*Uses* 34). And it might not always work to confirm the reader's perspective but instead to jar it loose: recognition can be "akin to seeing an unattractive, scowling, middle-aged person coming into a restaurant, only to suddenly realize that you have been looking into a mirror behind the counter and that this unappealing-looking person is you. Mirrors do not always flatter; they can take us off our guard, pull us up short, reflect our image in unexpected ways and from unfamiliar angles" (48). Even more than mirrors, in fact, Elizabeth Long suggests that characters with which readers identify might serve as prisms, leading to an "interrogation of self, other selves, and society beyond the text" (153). "Mere identification" is thus not only a more complex readerly act than it may appear; it might also provide an important starting point for the analytical forms of questioning and engagement that scholars hope to inspire.

In her study of Houston-area book clubs, Long focuses less on the transformative potential of reading for the individual than on the ways that reading's effects might be mediated and magnified by group discussions about books. The move toward a collective reckoning with the meanings produced in the reading process inevitably complicates those meanings, as reading group members are required to interact with the readings and life experiences of others. It is in these social negotiations that identification and the individualistic brand of empathy that it can inspire has the potential to grow into a generous, ethical engagement with self, other, and world. Such a developing sense of ethical engagement is among the best of what the university might be able to offer, both to its students and to the public: a demonstration of the ways that something as commonplace as the novel can become what Arthur Krystal calls a "tool for survival," a means of establishing and celebrating "an awareness of the human condition, which is both communal and individual and inevitably strikes a balance, palpable or barely perceptible, between the two." If one function that literature serves in individual readers' lives is opening in them the desire for intersubjective understanding, and if such desire can be built upon in communal settings to create a readiness for ethical political and social engagement, then not only do literary scholars have an obligation of sorts to support that work, but we should also want to participate in it. But participating does not mean directing. Ronald Grele argued as far back as 1981 that the work of the public historian should focus less on instructing the public about history than on enabling the public to do their own history. So with public literary criticism: the scholar's role might ideally be not to instruct others about the meaning of books but instead to enable them to develop and engage with those meanings themselves. And as Sharon Leon noted in the prepublication discussion of this book, "All of this work requires us to be willing to slow down and dwell in the space of engagement." It's a challenging task, but an important one, since it is through such participation that we can begin to demonstrate the importance of the academy to the entirety of the social enterprise.

Reading and the Social

There may at first glance appear something odd in the suggestion that reading—understood today as a deeply private, individual act, generally conducted in and productive of relative isolation from the world—could have such a profound connection to the social. Reading has not always been a private endeavor, however, and as the example of the book club (not to mention the classroom) might suggest, it isn't always undertaken alone today. As a result, I want to dig a bit further into the role that the social has long played in the reading process, as well as the contemporary relationship between reading and community. Reading serves for many readers as the ground for connection not only with authors and characters but also with one another. Avid readers often engage not just with texts but through texts, following and participating in public discussions about texts. In fact, the public literary criticism that I just invoked stretches far beyond the officially sanctioned channels of the *New York Times* and the *New York Review of Books* to include a wide variety of independent literary publications like *Electric Lit* and *The Millions,* as well as a vast amount of reader-generated criticism posted to discussion forums and email lists, to individual and group blogs, and to book-centered social networks like *Goodreads*. These critical discussions demonstrate enormous energy circulating around books, and the discussions themselves are followed by many more readers than actually participate in them. And beyond criticism, many readers produce their own creative fanworks that extend or revise the narrative universes they care about, and in the process they build extended fan communities, reading and discussing one another's work and creating deep social connections through their texts. The public nature of all of this discussion about reading, and the communities that develop among readers, suggest the social potential that reading together presents—a social potential that scholars and their institutions would do well to take seriously and to support.

Alberto Manguel, in *A History of Reading*, recounts the gradual shift in reading practices from public (out loud, authority-led, common) to private (silent, individuated, personal). That shift brought with it a host of freedoms, both actual and imagined: "A book that can be read privately, reflected upon as the eye unravels the sense of the words, is no longer subject to immediate clarification or guidance, condemnation or censorship by a listener. Silent reading allows unwitnessed communication between the book and the reader" (51). The solitary reader is free to form attachments and interpretations at will, and can connect meanings across texts in an unfettered and—in both a resolutely positive and a potentially dangerous sense—undisciplined fashion. It is no accident, then, that church history is replete with associations between silent reading and heresy; private reading posed, and poses, a direct threat to all manner of orthodoxy. On the other hand, as Manguel goes on to note, while "the ceremony of being read to no doubt deprives the listener of some of the freedom inherent in the act of reading . . . it also gives the versatile text a respectable identity, a sense of unity in time and an existence in space that it seldom has in the capricious hands of a solitary reader" (123). That sense of unity derived from experiences of social reading reaches beyond the text to affect the relationships between the reader and those being read to, as well as the relationships among those who read together. Though the freedoms and pleasures of reading have flourished in private, a continuing if noncoercive attention to the public aspects of reading can help support its role in developing and sustaining community.

Even the most private, solitary act of reading involves establishing and sustaining a relationship between the reader and the writer, however imaginary or constructed that relationship may prove. The work of creating that relationship is no less a goal of the writer than of the reader; as Alan Jacobs has noted, writers "publish at least in part because we want a personal connection. The more positive that connection the better, of course, but it must be human." That the connection required must be "human" indicates the reader's extensive agency in building a relationship with the author. Rather than simply evidence of being manipulated or led, this connection to the author demonstrates "something independently thoughtful and constructive in the reader's response" (*Pleasures* 54). And that independent thought process, though conducted internally, is never fully individual; it reflects and manifests the reader's desire for relationship with and connection to the world.

The mediated nature of readers' connections, however, renders them prone to being considered illusory. Deidre Lynch argues, for instance, that the eighteenth century "witnessed various projects intended to affirm the humanity that was lodged in the artifacts of the book market and thus to close some of the gaps between the living world and the paper world" (31), inventing connections that were a necessary condition of the market-based project of establishing what we now understand as the love of literature. However contrived in their anthropomorphism these projects were, they succeeded in far-reaching ways: readers today continue to find in bound volumes of ink-on-paper (or more recently, in digital files displayed on handheld devices) vibrant connections to authors and to characters. Whether scholars and other literary professionals understand those figures of apparent connection to be mere functions constructed by the text does not, on a most pragmatic level, matter. For many readers, these connections are real enough to produce significant personal responses.

Moreover, readers have the potential to move beyond such textually constructed relationships with authors or characters and to forge connections with a larger community of readers. At times this community is, in Benedict Anderson's sense, imagined: a reader identifies as a reader (or as a reader of some particular author, or some particular text) and thus feels part of a group whose members he or she will likely never meet. Kuisma Korhonen argues that this "invisible textual community" may well be "the most radical community of all: those who do not know each other, who are not reading for any clearly determined purpose, who open themselves to the otherness of literary texts beyond all socially shared conventions of interpretation." But that openness, when mediated through in-person or networked forms of communication, can allow for the creation of new kinds of communities that are something more than a mere textual effect. That is to say, connected communities of readers—from Anne Gere's turn-of-the-century women's groups, to Elizabeth Long's book clubs, to friends connected on *Goodreads*, and to fandoms linked in person and online—sharing with one another the thoughtful and constructive responses that enable them to build relationships with texts and authors, have a social potential that exceeds the boundaries of reading alone.

These communities of readers and the connections that they build with their texts and with one another demonstrate the potential of reading's very real impact on lives lived both singly and in relation to others. And the relationship between the impact of reading on the individual life and that on the larger community should not be dismissed. Timothy Aubry argues, for instance, that books that appeal to the therapeutic paradigm—those books, in other words, that we would most expect to encourage an inward, individualistic attitude—in fact have the potential to bring readers out of a solipsistic focus on their own internal lives and to facilitate what he calls "disaggregated solidarities of affect" (202). In other words, the kinds of identification and relation that provide much of mainstream reading practices' pleasure can also provide the basis for more outwardly oriented networks of intersubjective support.

Reading groups provide one obvious manifestation of and location for such support. As Long's study indicates, these groups not only create the space in which the readers who participate in them can "confront the wider changes they perceive around them and their own personal wishes, fears, dreams, and regrets," but they also establish "a deliberative space that encourages reflective awareness of this process" (176). This reflective awareness can be transformative both for individuals and for groups, as the interpretations and analyses that members of reading groups share promote "a clearer articulation of partially formed perceptions and implicit assumptions, whether about a specific book or about personal experience" (187). In working out these perceptions and assumptions together, in other words, readers have the potential to open themselves to other responses and other subject positions, thereby creating important connections both within the group and to the broader social world.

The reading group experience has been most famously expanded and mediated by Oprah's Book Club, which connected discussions ordinarily relegated to private rooms and granted a degree of visibility to Korhonen's invisible textual community. As Ted Striphas has argued in his exploration of this unlikely relationship between the television empire and the publishing world, the success of Oprah's Book Club derived in no small degree from its practice of tailoring the reading experience to the actual audience that the show hoped to reach, a pragmatic approach that "engages actual and potential readers at the level of the everyday" (138). To reach its audience, to engage them in the discussions about books that the show's producers wished to have, Oprah's Book Club was required not just to select good books, but to find the right books for its readers—and, even more, to find clear, compelling ways to communicate to those readers that the book selected was the right book for them. The explicitly educational goals of the book club resulted in a more complex relationship to viewer desire than we might ordinarily grant to television, that most commercial of platforms. The book club's audience sought a compelling reading experience within which they felt some personal connection. As Oprah indicated in an interview given in the last days of her show, the program's overarching objective was "to let the viewer know that whatever you're going through, you're not alone" (Stelter). Beyond Oprah, however, the flourishing communities of readers online, and the writing they do with and for one another, enable readers to find one another more directly, and to transform their reading into something more.

This is not to say, however, that all connections forged through the discussion of books are necessarily productive or enlightening, or that they serve the progressive ends for which we might hope. In-person book groups are very often homogenous and can work to reinforce the status quo, however good their intentions might be. When faced with challenges, these groups can all too readily leave the difficult work of imaginative connection behind in favor of more solipsistic exploration. Long has noted as well that existing social dynamics are not erased in the space of the book group. These groups can carve out a safe space in which the exploration of new questions about the relationship between self and world can be raised, but they can also all too easily silence such questioning through "informal processes of social control" including "joking and a lack of responsiveness," which result in an enforced social conformity (187). These same dynamics, however, exist within the college classroom, and perhaps the most important role that instructors play is noticing those tendencies where they occur, calling attention to them when it is productive to do so, and rerouting discussion in more generous directions. While there are better and worse ways to imagine scholars playing a similar role in off-campus settings, this expertise could nonetheless be used (in conjunction with the kinds of listening discussed in the previous chapter) to help shape intellectually and emotionally productive informal group reading experiences. Not least, the work that instructors do in the classroom can serve as a model that empowers other readers to carry forward these practices into to their own community discussions.

If scholars are to participate in extramural reading groups, however, it is crucial that we recognize the ways that our interventions can easily derail conversations and demoralize their participants. We must approach these encounters as occasions on which we have more to learn than we do to teach, or as opportunities, in Hochschild's memorable phrase, to "scale the empathy wall" that separates those whose worldviews are so radically disparate that mutual understanding seems impossible. Such an empathy wall, as I've suggested, separates scholars from general-interest readers, and building the possibility of connection across it is of paramount importance. Recent studies in cognitive science seem to indicate a link at the neurological level between reading fiction and the development of empathy. Though it is not entirely clear, as discussed in chapter 1, that this model of empathy is necessarily a good thing, these studies suggest that readers have more developed abilities to imagine the thoughts and feelings of others, a capability that may play a key role in social relationships. Settings in which reading provides a basis for discussion with others whose interpretations may be different can perhaps create an important space in which those abilities can be tested and extended into generosity and compassion. And that goes for scholars as well: we can be part of that process, but only if we are willing to be genuine participants, to recognize the ways our own potential for empathy, for generosity, might develop in the encounter.

We must recognize this, because whatever cognitive scientists may be discovering about the brain's functioning, genuine empathy is no simple mechanistic matter, and its development often requires moments of painful failure and always requires difficult, humbling work. And it is crucial work: while I've argued earlier in this chapter that the processes of identification in which many readers engage should not be so readily dismissed as superficial, identification as a mechanism for reading works best when it leads to something beyond recognition of the self, to the beginnings of a more broadly social understanding. In fact, a too-simple sense of recognition presents real dangers for that understanding. As Dominic LaCapra has noted, uncritical identification can result in "the derivation of one's identity from others in ways that deny their otherness" (83), by assuming that a shared feeling can eliminate real difference. This mode of identification not only promotes an essentialist model of selfhood—assuming an identity between self and other—but also runs the risk of colonizing the other's experience as one's own, whether by taking over the other's perspective or by projecting one's own perspective onto the other. The reader engaging with work that actively courts an emotional connection needs to become critically aware of the effects of simplistic modes of identification, acknowledging, as LaCapra suggests, "one's own opacities and gaps that prevent full identity or self-knowledge" (77). In so doing, the reader can enact a more ethical form of empathic identification, remaining open to the other's otherness while nonetheless experiencing the emotional connection.

That is to say, scholars are right to be wary of the particular mode of identification that is promoted in many in-person reading groups as well as in mediated settings like Oprah's Book Club, but not because of the appeal to identification itself. Rather, the problem is that the kind of engagement with characters and situations espoused by the book club is too often grounded in a romantic, narcissistic version of identification predicated on the obliteration of difference and working toward the ultimate goal of self-acceptance. Alison Landsberg describes this mode of connection as sympathy rather than empathy, arguing that sympathy "presumes sameness between the sympathizer and her object, whether or not there is actually a 'sameness' between them," and that this presumption results in a mode of reading in which "one projects one's own feelings onto another" (149). This is a mode of reading that requires a "relatable" text, one that can be simply incorporated into one's worldview without requiring change in response. Empathy, by contrast with sympathy, is often painful. As

LaCapra notes, it should not be understood as "an incorporation of the other into one's own (narcissistic) self" but should instead should provoke a recognition of "one's internal alterity or difference from oneself" (76–77). Genuine empathy, in other words, results in self-questioning rather than self-confirmation. Where many reading groups, including large-scale projects like Oprah's Book Club, seem to fall short is in focusing on personal growth rather than more complex modes of ethical engagement.

Ethical engagement with a text or with a community—a mode of engagement that encourages a critical awareness of difference and that promotes questioning rather than conclusion—can be a hallmark of the academy, but only if we are willing to open ourselves to the same questioning we ask of others. It's for this reason that Bill Readings, in describing the ethical practices that underwrite teaching and learning, draws on Maurice Blanchot's conception of the obligation members of an ethical community owe one another: "an infinite attention to the other" (qtd in Readings 161). That infinite attention, as we saw in the last chapter, takes the form, first and foremost, of listening, but it's a kind of listening that requires us not simply to take on board new information but to question what we already know. That is to say, in our engagements with texts and with other readers, we must grapple not only with the stories that others tell us, but with the parts of ourselves that resist or rewrite those stories. And this work is necessarily difficult: as Aubry describes Toni Morrison's *Paradise*, the "central project in the novel is to construct, with the help of the reader, new utopian models based on the negotiation between author and reader, and this joint venture of collectively envisioning and producing paradise will necessarily be a difficult, endless task" (49).

The question that remains: How can we inspire both ourselves and others to remain committed to this endless task? How might scholars who care about literature, or history, or art, or philosophy, or any of the many subjects studied within the contemporary university, work to encourage general-interest readers to engage in the kinds of difficult reading and interpretation that the production of Morrison's paradise requires? Is there a potential relationship that can be forged between the reader's desire for identification and self-discovery in the text and a more challenging exploration of otherness? As Ann Jurecic has noted, readers do not automatically become "attuned to others" (12) in the act of reading; empathy, she argues, "is not salvation; it's not certainty or knowledge; it blurs boundaries in ways that can be both generative and destructive. In the end, empathy is a practice, a process that extends in time. To make it work takes both effort and humility" (22). As we noted in the last chapter, practices, by their nature, must be practiced: no one is good at them right off the bat. Readers of all varieties, then, have the opportunity to practice the kinds of empathy that can help them become better readers—and to practice the kinds of reading that can help them develop more generative forms of empathy—precisely by reading together, by wrestling collectively with texts and their interpretation.

Doing so will require all of us, readers both inside and outside the academy, to be honest with ourselves about what we hope to gain from our participation in modes of social reading such as book groups. As Korhonen notes,

There are many good (and many not so good) reasons to read and to participate in actual working communities of readers: we may gain cultural capital, we may develop our emotional skills,

we may learn more about other cultures, we may satisfy our curiosity, we may enjoy voyeurism, we may just want to kill time,
etc. (Or, as professionals of literature, we may gain money.) But
for the most part, these "reasons" imply that there is some other,
more fundamental desire for reading, desire that cannot be pin-
pointed or defined exactly, except perhaps by this loose and not
really very clear definition: we read because we are not self-
sufficient creatures, because we acknowledge (perhaps uncon-
sciously) the imperative of the Other, the necessity to stay open
to the call of otherness.

Academic readers might fulfill this call by demonstrating our own
lack of self-sufficiency, by stepping outside the teacher role and
practicing alongside other kinds of readers, staying open to what
they may have to teach us.

Readers and Scholars

That having been said, scholars also have some talents that we
might bring to public reading projects, not least a commitment
to questioning, to analysis, and to concern for detail, as well as a
knowledge base that allows us to see and draw connections across
texts. These talents, used in the classroom, help draw students into
our subject matter; they might be similarly used to help general-
interest readers pursue their own reading interests and discover
the peculiar pleasures of the professionalized reading practices engaged in on university campuses. If scholars could find ways to
involve the public not just in what we read or how we read but
also *why* we read the ways we read, we might be able to encourage greater understanding of and interest in the kinds of learning that goes on in our fields.

Too many of us have had the experience of having someone—a student, a family member, a friend—tell us, sometimes pityingly and nearly always with frustration, that we're "reading too much into" something or that we're taking all the joy out of some cultural experience. That joyless too-muchness characterizes scholarly reading for many outside the profession, and it might be worth thinking a bit about how scholars actually read if we're going to find ways to counteract that association. John Guillory, in a paper exploring reading as an ethical practice, describes scholarly or professional reading as having four peculiar characteristics:

> First of all, it is a kind of *work,* a labor requiring large amounts of time and resources. This labor is compensated as such, by a salary. Second, it is a *disciplinary* activity, that is, it is governed by conventions of interpretation and protocols of research developed over many decades. These techniques take years to acquire; otherwise we would not award higher degrees to those who succeed in mastering them. Third, professional reading is *vigilant;* it stands back from the experience of pleasure in reading, not in order to cancel out this pleasure but in order necessarily to be wary of it, so that the experience of reading does not begin and end in the pleasure of consumption, but gives rise to a certain sustained reflection. And fourth, this reading is a *communal* practice. Even when the scholar reads in privacy, this act of reading is connected in numerous ways to communal scenes; and it is often dedicated to the end of a public and publishable "reading." (31–32)

Guillory contrasts these characteristics with those he ascribes to "lay reading," which is "practiced at the site of *leisure,*" operates under very different *"conventions,"* is "motivated by the experience of *pleasure,"* and is "largely a *solitary* practice" (32). Certain of these characteristics seem indisputable: that the conventions of professional reading are disciplinary in function is apparent, and that the purpose of professional reading is work rather than leisure is a key aspect of what makes it professional. But there's much to contest otherwise. Given, on the one hand, the proliferation of in-person and online reading communities and, on the other, the professorial attachment to more monastic encounters with the object of study, I might suggest that the communal/solitary labels could easily be inverted. And, perhaps most importantly, the distinction drawn between vigilance and pleasure misses the extent to which avid readers scour their chosen texts for detail, as well as the very real pleasures that lead scholars to read the ways they do. Guillory later acknowledges that such pleasure "subsists unrecognized" in professional reading (42), but if, as he argues, it's necessary to a healthy public sphere for "the cultures of intellectual expertise" and the cultures of lay readership to "communicate across the gap" (43), we need to do a much better job of exploring and explaining the pleasures of scholarly reading.

After all, it's not that there aren't real pleasures in a mode of reading that might be characterized as "vigilant"; there absolutely are. It's more that the pleasures of vigilance are different. For confirmation of just how different they can be, one might look to Roland Barthes, whose notions of the pleasure of the text seem to bear more rupture, unsettlement, loss, struggle, and even combat than they do the kinds of absorption that are conventionally associated with enjoyment: "What I enjoy in a narrative," Barthes confides, "is not directly its content or even its structure, but rather the abrasions I impose upon the fine surface" (11–12). Barthes highlights the traces of the sadistic in the scholarly relationship to the text, certainly, but in these abrasions—or perhaps inscriptions—there is the potential for great pleasure. And it's a pleasure that readers who participate in online reading communities and fandoms are highly likely to understand: the joy of finding meaning in a text, of marking that meaning, and of writing your own interpretation into it.

As in Barthes's case, some of that pleasure derives from mastery, from control, from transforming the text that is being read into the reader's own response. And sometimes the sense of mastery derives from uncovering that which the text does not want uncovered, the dirty little secrets that lurk beneath its surface. This highly rewarding mode of academic reading is associated with what Paul Ricoeur famously called the "hermeneutics of suspicion," a mode of interpretation that seeks out the buried truths of representation. Scholars including Eve Sedgwick and Rita Felski have explored the ways that this mode can result in a reading experience that blurs pleasure and pain. For Sedgwick, suspicion easily devolves into paranoia, a mode that bears a deep "aversion to surprise" and that finally "cements the intimacy between paranoia and knowledge per se" (130). The problem is of course that what the paranoid knows is mostly the stuff of paranoia itself: the reader caught up in paranoid knowledge is trapped by its "practice of disavowing its affective motive and force and masquerading as the very stuff of truth" (138). Felski, rather than focusing on the pain of paranoia, instead points to the role of guilt in driving scholars' suspicious reading practices: "Only by acting like detectives— interrogating and cross-examining the texts of culture—can we avoid being mistaken for criminals (those accused of political quietism, active complicity, or worse)" (*Limits* 118). Criticism thus becomes a means by which scholars declare their innocence, separating themselves from the guilty culture by which they are surrounded.

Paranoia and guilt are of course extremes; most scholarly reading practices do not so closely approach the pathological. But if those extremes tell us something about the ways that scholars read, they might also lead us to ask whether they are implicated in scholars' alienation from the broader reading public. If our ways of reading seem joyless to general readers, might there be ways for us to demonstrate where their pleasures lie? Felski notes that we do not, by and large, feel joyless about our work, but we are routinely called upon to perform a particular kind of critical detachment in the service of seriousness. This seriousness is often held to be opposed to enthusiasm; too much enthusiasm—not just among critics, but among novelists as well, as Emma Straub discovered when she became the leading example in Jacob Silverman's "Against Enthusiasm"—and one runs the risk of being thought overly nice, shallow, and part of a "mutual admiration society" having "a chilling effect on literary culture" (Silverman). Straub herself went on to celebrate her enthusiasm in part by noting that she is not a critic, but Felski suggests that opposing "critical detachment and amateur enthusiasm" in the ways that both Silverman and Straub do "fails to do justice to the mixed motives and complicated passions that drive academic argument" (*Limits* 152). Our relationships with the texts we study are often fraught, but perhaps in demonstrating the care that we bring to our critical work, we might better reveal why that work inspires us, and we might encourage others to join us in the project.

I want to emphasize that I do not think that critique per se is the problem, or the thing that alienates general-interest readers from academic readers. In fact, as all those reading-oriented networks demonstrate, avid readers can be quite fierce and discerning critics, and fans' transformations of the characters and storylines in fictional universes often demonstrate a critical interest in bringing to the surface what the original text has repressed. Instead, what separates scholars from other readers, whether our students or readers off-campus, is professionalization. Even this, however, is not to say that professionalization *per se* is the problem; mine is not a call for the elimination of the role of the expert. Rather, as Gerald Graff notes in his history of the profession of literature, the issue lies in "the specific forms professionalism has taken under the peculiar circumstances of the new university, forms which—it must be stressed—need not be the only forms possible" (5). Those forms early on required the teaching of literature— often assumed to teach itself—to demonstrate its rigor as a field of scientific inquiry in order to justify its place on the American campus. And that justification is key; it underwrites the series of conflicts that Graff explores in the history of literary studies: "classicists versus modern-language scholars; research investigators versus generalists; historical scholars versus critics; New Humanists versus New Critics; academic critics versus literary journalists and culture critics; critics and scholars versus theorists" (14). These conflicts are the very shape of the professional as it has evolved on campus over the last century-plus, a shape that is today overdetermined by the internalized competitive structures of contemporary life as a whole. That need to be competitive, as it manifests within the university, leads scholars to adopt pugilistic forms of critique, as well as styles of discourse that exclude the uninitiated, as the primary modes of engagement with our work. These modes allow us not only to demonstrate our dominance over the materials that we study and the ways that those who've gone before us have studied them, but also to establish and maintain our standing within the academic marketplace.

The solution, if we are to find one, is likely to require a significant rethinking of the institutional values and structures that determine the ways we work on campus; I'll dig into that rethinking in the final chapter. But it will also likely include an ethical, caring embrace of our more positive enthusiasms for the materials we study. Such enthusiasm feels dangerous today; we run the risk of being taken for the weak, superficial, or even ideologically complicit reader Jameson decried. Enthusiasm feels unprofessional, surfacing a dangerous association with the amateur; Lynch, as discussed earlier, has explored at length the risks involved in requiring scholars to perform their love of literature, as that enthusiasm threatens to deprofessionalize the field and devalue the labor that goes into it. Enthusiasm, as Graff might note, risks the assumption that our fields can teach themselves. And yet, as Catharine Stimpson has argued, our concern with professionalization has become disordered; while we "humanists tell truth to power and tell truths about power, we disregard the balancing activity of serving as witnesses for the humanities and their affirmations. We are embarrassed by or frightened of or skeptical about or ironic about the humanities as the place where we—whether we are professional humanists or not—demonstrate our loves—our loves of authors, of texts, of the imagination in action, of wisdom" (14). The result is all too clear: "If we do not love our work, why should anyone else care?" (15). Finding ways to demonstrate what we love about our work may, in fact, help us demonstrate what is important about our work without requiring us to do so through competition.

What readers love about reading, and the impact that it can have on their lives, is relatively clear: reading of a wide range of types of texts has the power to open us to other perspectives, to other experiences, to other lives, to create a connection between our private selves and the public sphere. Reading can help encourage the development, however preliminary, of the kind of inter-subjective understanding necessary to the creation and sustenance of difficult structures of community. Contemporary literary criticism, like the forms of reading that take place in many fields across university campuses, has much to offer to that process—not least, deepening identification and sympathy into more complex, more ethically engaged forms of empathy and generosity—but only if that criticism can engage the same communities of readers: the students who might be drawn to our fields; the life-long readers who might help support our institutions and the work we do within them. For scholars to begin to forge connections with those readers, we must be willing to demonstrate our love for our work, to open our reading processes to others, to invite them into open exchange with us, to engage them directly in the hows and whys of our approaches to our fields. Creating an environment in which the public might begin to care about our work demands that we do at least some of that work in public—the subject of the next chapter.

3

Working in Public

If democracy is to mean anything at all, then experts and laypeople have to solve complicated problems together. First, however, they have to overcome the widening gulf between them.

—TOM NICHOLS, *THE DEATH OF EXPERTISE*

started blogging in 2002, fairly early in the academic scheme of things. I'd just finished the long process of rewriting the thing that had been my dissertation, turning it into my first book, and I was feeling a little stifled: all that work, years of work, were encapsulated in a Word document that existed on my hard disk, in several backups, and nowhere else, and there seemed the very real possibility that no one might ever read it. And then I stumbled across the blog of a friend from grad school who had moved out of a teaching position to work for a web-based company. His blog was funny and erudite, exploring recent books and culture and bits of anecdote. And *it had an audience.* People read it, and I knew they read it because they left brief comments responding to and interacting with the author, offering their own thoughts and amplifying his. And I thought, wow, that's it.

My blog, *Planned Obsolescence,* which I started out of the baldest desire to get someone somewhere to read something I wrote, wound up doing something more interesting than I expected: it didn't just build an audience—it built a community. I found a number of other early academic bloggers, all of whom linked to one another, commented on each other's posts, and responded at greater length with posts of their own. Among those bloggers was a small cluster of folks who came out of literary studies—the Wordherders, a blogging collective whose platform was provided by a grad student at the University of Maryland, who worked at the Maryland Institute for Technology and the Humanities: Jason Rhody. Jason and the other Wordherders (including Lisa Rhody, George Williams, Chuck Tryon, Kari Kraus, Matt Kirschenbaum, and Vika Zafrin, among others) became my first real online colleagues, and we remain connected today.

Those relationships, which opened out into a growing network of scholars working online, were crucial to me as an assistant professor at a small liberal arts college on the far end of the country. I had spent the previous few years feeling isolated, my work by and large unknown, and I could not figure out how to make the intellectual and professional connections that might help my writing develop and find an audience. *Planned Obsolescence* helped build those connections—and it appears that posts I published there were the first pieces of my writing to be cited in formal academic settings. The blog was read, by people in my field, and by people in other fields altogether.

Fast-forward to the moment in 2009 when I'd just finished the draft of my second book, not-so-coincidentally entitled *Planned Obsolescence.* The thing I was supposed to do—the thing our usual processes provide for—was to send it off to the press, which would commission two or three experts to review it and suggest improvements before publication. I did that, of course, but my press also agreed to let me post the draft online for open comment.

In the years since, I've been asked about that decision a lot—whether it was worth the risk and how I managed to work up the courage to release something unfinished into the world where anyone could have said anything about it. My answers to these questions are not wholly satisfying, I fear; the truth of the matter is that the risks really didn't figure into my thinking. What I knew was that there were a lot of folks out there, in a lot of different kinds of jobs in a wide range of fields, with whom I'd had productive, engaging interactions that contributed to the book's development, and I really wanted to hear their thoughts about where I'd wound up. I trusted them to help me—and they did, overwhelmingly so.

It's important to acknowledge the entire boatload of privilege that not-thinking about the risks requires. I was writing from a sufficiently safe position that allowing flaws in my work-in-progress to be publicly visible wasn't a real threat. I was free to model an open process not least because of the job security that comes with tenure, but also because I'd been in that open process all along; much of the book grew out of blog posts and public talks that had already produced a lot of discussion, and so I had a sense of how readers might respond. Beyond this, though, it's not at all incidental that it was 2009, not 2018—a much more idealistic, open, trusting hour in the age of the internet. The events of the last few years, from GamerGate to the 2016 presidential campaign and beyond, have made the risks involved in opening one's work up online all too palpable. But my experiences with the blog, with the book manuscript, and with other projects I've opened to online discussion nonetheless leave me convinced that there is a community, existing or potential, interested in the kind of work I care about, willing to engage with and support that work's development. And—perhaps most importantly today—willing to work on building and sustaining the community itself.

This chapter focuses on the ways that working in public, and with the public, can enable scholars to build that kind of community, both within their fields, with other scholars in different fields, and with folks off campus who care about the kinds of work that we do. By finding ways to connect with readers and writers beyond our usual circles of experts, in a range of different registers, and in ways that move beyond enabling *them* to listen to *us* to instead allow for meaningful dialogue and collaboration, we can create the possibilities for far more substantial public participation in and engagement with a wide range of kinds of academic work. We can build programs and networks and platforms that do not just bring the university to the world, but also involve the world in the university.

There are, of course, several real obstacles that have to be faced in this process. Some of them reflect the shifting and proliferating communication platforms that we use today. Blogs, for instance, do not receive quite the same focus that they did in the early 2000s, and their posts do not receive the same kinds of comments. In part, this decline in attention comes as the result of what a friend of mine refers to as "catastrophic success"; there is such an overwhelming number of blogs and blog-like online publications today that the audience is of necessity dispersed, fragmented, and distracted. And the distractions, of course, come not just from the explosion in the quantity of "content" available online but from the effects of their publishers' quest for revenue— the ads and other intrusions that today render many online publications all but unreadable. The relative drop in blog-based interaction can also be traced to the decline and death of a few related technologies that kept readers aware of what was happening on their favorite sites, most significantly Google Reader, a highly used personalizable aggregator that enabled users to keep up with the blogs they cared about. And that drop has been exacerbated as the discussions that blog posts engendered have in many cases spun off of the blogs themselves and onto Twitter and Facebook and other networks where readers engage with one another rather than with the author. As a result, online communities of readers and writers are unlikely to develop spontaneously, as they seemed to in the early 2000s; instead, we need to be deliberate in reaching out to potential readers and participants where they are, finding ways to draw them, and ourselves, back into sustained conversation.

And of course the nature of internet discourse has changed in recent years as much as has its location. Trolls are not a new phenomenon, by any means, but they certainly seem to have multiplied, and the damage that they can inflict has escalated. In the weeks before I started drafting this chapter, an assistant professor received numerous rape and death threats based on a political website's mischaracterizations of a column she published online; an adjunct faculty member was fired by her institution for remarks she made in a televised interview with a particularly goading host; and an associate professor was suspended for sharing a controversial online article on Twitter, using a blunt phrase drawn from the article as a hashtag in the process. The visibility involved in taking one's work public can produce significant risk—especially where that work involves questions of social justice, which are under attack by malevolent groups online, and especially for people of color, women, and other already marginalized and underrepresented members of the academic community whose every engagement is met by a hostile world.

I do not have the answers to these problems; though I have worked on the development of a number of online communities, I do not have a perfect platform to offer, and I do not know how to repair the malignant aspects of human behavior. I am convinced, however, that countering these destructive forces will require advance preparation and focused responses; as Tressie McMillan Cottom has argued, attacks like these are an organized effort, and academics must be organized, too ("Academic Outrage"). Ensuring that public engagement surrounding our work remains productive will require a tremendous amount of collective labor, and the careful development and maintenance of trust, in order to create inclusive online communities that can be open to, and yet safe in, the world. But there are several other challenges as well, challenges that are less about the state of the internet and more about the ways that we as scholars do our work, and ways that we can draw a range of broader publics to that work, that I want to dig further into in what follows.

The first is the need to ensure that the work we do can be discovered and accessed by any interested reader, and not just by those readers who have ready entry to well-funded research libraries. It should go without saying that it is impossible for anyone to care about what we do if they cannot see it. And yet, perhaps because we assume we are mostly writing for one another, the results of our work end up overwhelmingly in places where it cannot be found—and even if it is found, where it cannot be accessed—by members of the broader public. Making our work more available is the first step in creating a richer connection with readers outside our inner circles, readers who might not only care about what we do but be encouraged to support it.

The second step lies in ensuring that the work is accessible in a very different sense: not just allowing readers to get their hands on it, but enabling them to see in it the things that they might care about. Academic writers often resent the ways that the work they do gets mainstreamed without appropriate credit in popular publishing venues (one might see a discussion of this phenomenon, and its accompanying resentment, in Amanda Ann Klein and Kristin Warner's "Erasing the Pop-Culture Scholar, One Click at a Time"), but a key part of the problem is of course that those academic writers do not do the mainstreaming themselves. We ought to be thinking about ways to ensure that we communicate our arguments—and especially those arguments with broad public interest or implications—in order to engage readers where they are, rather than always forcing them to come find us, in our venues and on our terms.

Finally, and perhaps most importantly, if we hope to engage the public with our work, we need to ensure that it is open in the broadest possible sense: open to response, to participation, to more new thought, more new writing, and more kinds of cultural creation by more kinds of public scholars. In other words, we need to think not just about the public's potential consumption of the work that is done by the university, but also about potential new modes of co-production that involve the surrounding communities in the work of the university. These rich, ongoing collaborations might serve as a style of work that our universities can fruitfully model for the rest of our culture: new modes of interaction, new forms of public engagement, and new kinds of writing not just for, but with the world.

My focus in this chapter, then, is on the ways that we might facilitate greater public interaction for scholars and scholarship. To some extent, this involves making the work that scholars do more publicly accessible, and to some extent, it involves helping scholars understand the potential for their work to enter into dialogue with a range of publics. In part, then, I want to expand the ways we distribute scholarship today, but I also want us to think about the ways that scholars address that scholarship to one another and about the communities that we form in the process. When I say that scholars' work might address or engage a broader set of publics, I do not mean to suggest that there is no place for internal exchange among field-based experts; there is, and should be. But there should also be means for the results of those exchanges to become part of the larger cultural conversations taking place around us. And when I indicate the multiplicity of that "broader set of publics," I mean to steer us away from a sense of the public's singularity. I do not mean that our work needs to address or engage everyone, at all times; rather, different aspects of our work might reach different publics at different moments. Knowing how to think respectfully about those audiences—and, indeed, to think about them not just as audiences, but as potential interlocutors—is a crucial skill for the twenty-first-century academic.

Public Access

This begins in the simplest possible way: ensuring that the readers we might hope to reach have access to the work that we're already doing, in the forms that we're already doing it. A number of related initiatives are working concurrently to make the entirety of the research process more shared and shareable, including the open-notebook science and open-data movements, but the greatest traction and the greatest potential for transformation across the disciplines has thus far emerged from the open-access publishing movement. Mobilization around the establishment of open access began in the scientific community more than twenty years ago, and has since spread, with varying degrees of uptake, to all academic fields. The conditions for this movement's development were, at the outset, economic: scientific journal subscription prices had risen precipitously in the early 1990s (and have continued escalating since), creating both a crisis for research library budgets and a growing information divide between those with access to such libraries and those without. In order to create a more globally equitable distribution of knowledge, scientists began to debate and organize around a set of possibilities for transforming publishing processes and creating new models for opening scientific journal articles to everyone.

The goals of the open-access movement were never solely altruistic; it was clear even in its early days that science itself would benefit if its communication processes were freed from the commercial channels into which it was increasingly being funneled and access to the research literature were unencumbered. But the links between the social good created by increased public access to research results and the potential for accelerating scientific discovery were established early on. The Association of Research Libraries gathered a cluster of early listserv discussions around these issues into a 1995 volume entitled *Scholarly Journals at the Crossroads: A Subversive Proposal for Electronic Publishing*. In the introduction, editors Ann Shumelda Okerson and James J. O'Donnell argue that "in the interests of science, the law of the market *cannot* be allowed to function. An item with a very small market may yet be the indispensable link in a chain of research that leads to a result of high social value" (1). The escape from the market values that dominated scientific communication, in other words, would help science progress, and that progress could potentially serve the public good.

The open-access movement was thus established as a means of attempting to ensure that the social value served by scholarly research could flourish. The guiding principles of this movement were originally articulated in the Budapest Open Access Initiative, published in 2002, which gave the movement its name. Following behind the Budapest initiative were the June 2003 Bethesda Statement on Open Access Publishing and the October 2003 Berlin Declaration on Open Access to Scientific Knowledge. Together, Budapest-Bethesda-Berlin defined the agenda for open-access scholarly publishing:

> By "open access" to this literature, we mean its free availability on the public internet, permitting any users to read, download, copy, distribute, print, search, or link to the full texts of these articles, crawl them for indexing, pass them as data to software, or use them for any other lawful purpose, without financial, legal, or technical barriers other than those inseparable from gaining access to the internet itself. The only constraint on reproduction and distribution, and the only role for copyright in this domain, should be to give authors control over the integrity of their work and the right to be properly acknowledged and cited. (Chan et al.)

"Open access," that is, means free access not just in the sense of "gratis," work made available without charge, but also in the sense of "libre," work that, subject to appropriate scholarly standards of citation, is free to be built upon. This is the cornerstone of the scholarly project: scholarship is written to be read and to influence more new writing. Early mobilization around open access thus targeted not just the economic inequities that were being worsened by the market orientation of scientific publishers, but the resulting restrictions in the creation of new knowledge created by the growing divide between the information haves and have-nots. Open access presented the potential for scholars to help bridge this divide, serving not only their own interests in getting their work into broader circulation, but also a larger public interest.

As the Budapest Open Access Initiative put it:

> An old tradition and a new technology have converged to make possible an unprecedented public good. The old tradition is the willingness of scientists and scholars to publish the fruits of their research in scholarly journals without payment, for the sake of inquiry and knowledge. The new technology is the internet. The public good they make possible is the world-wide electronic distribution of the peer-reviewed journal literature and completely free and unrestricted access to it by all scientists, scholars, teachers, students, and other curious minds. Removing access barriers to this literature will accelerate research, enrich education, share the learning of the rich with the poor and the poor with the rich, make this literature as useful as it can be, and lay the foundation for uniting humanity in a common intellectual conversation and quest for knowledge. (Chan et al.)

It's hard not to be moved by the idealism of a statement such as this, and easy to see why the movement's impact accelerated. By the tenth anniversary of the Budapest Open Access Initiative, the open-access movement had spread widely through a dramatic increase in the number of OA journals (the so-called gold road to open access), including the very public resignations of a number of editorial boards of closed-access journals, who then joined together to start new publications online. Additionally, the open-access movement was profoundly expanded through a growing number of institutional and disciplinary repositories that collect the prepublication version of authors' manuscripts and other materials (the "green" road to open access), as well as an increasing number of institution- and funder-based mandates requiring the deposit of the products of research done under their auspices.

What made this growth in commitment to open access possible, as Peter Suber points out, is the precise convergence of the internet's ability to radically reduce the costs of reproduction and distribution of texts to near-zero with what Budapest calls the "old tradition" of scholars publishing their work without direct payment. That latter factor, Suber notes, "does more than insulate cutting-edge research from the market and free scholars to consent to OA without losing revenue. It also supports academic freedom and the kinds of serious inquiry that advance knowledge" (16). That scientists and other scholars are indirectly rewarded—with jobs, promotions, speaking engagements, and so forth—for the impact of their work rather than directly paid through sales means that they are free to "microspecialize," as Suber puts it, focusing their energies on areas that may be "of immediate interest to just a handful of people in the world, which are essential to pushing the frontiers of knowledge" (16). While some have argued that the public cannot understand and therefore does not need access to such highly specialized work, ensuring that everyone who might be interested is able to find and engage with this work precisely so that those frontiers can be pushed requires making it as fully and as freely available as possible. That is to say, the value of public access is not determined by the size of the potential public, just as the value of a scholarly field is not diminished by its relative smallness.

However, it is important to note that there have been some significant differences among fields in their abilities to embrace open access. Some of these differences have to do with the obviousness of public impact: the implications for medical research, for instance, in "uniting humanity" in a common quest for knowledge might be obvious, but the role that the humanities might play in contributing to and sustaining a "common intellectual conversation" has been a good bit less so. But some of the differences are more pragmatic in nature: the early open-access movement was clear from the beginning that its focus was on freeing journal articles from barriers to access. This is a relatively attainable goal, insofar as the incentives for authors (increased impact) outweigh, or should outweigh, the potential drawbacks (lost revenue or prestige), and the technologies available for circulating and reading articles online are well developed. In many fields in the humanities and social sciences, however, the most important work is done in book rather than article form. The technologies for circulating and reading books online have been to this point far less suitable to most research purposes; it's one thing to read and mark up a 20-page PDF file, but 200 pages of PDF—assuming that such a document can actually be obtained and loaded onto a decent reading device, which is a big assumption—reveals that format's discomforts and difficulties. Moreover, the incentives for book authors are slightly different, and differently delivered, than those for authors of journal articles. Book authors do receive royalties on the sale of their publications, and while the amount actually received may be modest, or even negligible, there remains at least an imagined potential that your book could be that fabled object, the cross-over book, that is reviewed in the *New York Times* and that sells beyond everyone's wildest expectations and that generates royalty checks capable of supporting more than a hamburger lunch.

Visible within that fantasy of entering into the mainstream book market, however, is a slightly countervailing incentive, one that is far and away the most important driver of book authors' publishing behavior: prestige. It is, after all, the *New York Times* whose review we dream of, and not some other rag. Perceived prestige drives many authors' choice of press with which they seek to publish, not least because of the reward structures presented by most research universities; at those institutions, a university-press published book is a requirement for tenure and promotion, and at the most prestigious universities, the press involved must be a "top" press (a somewhat murky and yet all-important designation). And while moving a highly selective scientific journal online has had no appreciable effects on its perceived prestige, given the ways that prestige is calculated, this is somewhat less true of journals in other, more print-oriented fields, and it is completely untrue of books. Scholars in those fields frequently feel a loss of prestige in any publication that does not result in a printed and bound object, and a book that is produced through such a nonconventional publishing system is frequently not considered to be a book at all. This isn't just a matter of a retrogressive, out-of-touch field that refuses to let go of its fetish object; it's about where scholars understand value to lie, and the incentives involved in pursuing that particular form of value. The existence of a book implies that a press, its external readers, and its board felt that the work contained within it was sufficiently important and of high enough quality to make it worth investing the resources required to produce it. The lower the required resources, the lower the value, and by association, the lower the apparent quality.

In other words, a widespread migration of book-based fields to an open-access publishing model has some significant challenges to face, and the financial and technological challenges may be the easiest among them. Lots of great projects are exploring those challenges, and they will likely lead to viable new models, as we might see in new publishers like Lever Press, Punctum Books, and Open Book Publishers; new open-access ventures at established presses, such as Luminos at the University of California Press; new platforms such as Manifold at the University of Minnesota Press and Fulcrum at the University of Michigan Press; new library-based efforts to support open access by providing both publishing services and open-access publishing funds; and new multi-institutional funding models such as the joint open-access monograph publishing initiative of the Association of American Universities, Association of Research Libraries, and Association of University Presses. The major challenge that isn't yet being fully accounted for, however, is the difficulty involved in changing human behavior, especially when it's behavior that has historically been tied to tangible rewards. All of which is to acknowledge that the open-access movement has met with some significant resistance and to argue that it's important for us to examine that resistance head-on, to think carefully about its implications for creating real public engagement with and public concern for the work that is done on campus.

I don't want to make it sound, however, as though all of the technical and financial challenges have been met, and that it's only scholars' recalcitrance or their institutions' backward reward systems that prevent the full embrace of open publishing across the disciplines. In fact, significant challenges remain for funding the open distribution of scholarship. The economic model into which much open-access publishing has settled in the last decade is, for instance, far more readily suited to the sciences and highly challenging to make work in the humanities and many branches of the social sciences. Rather than the traditional mode of funding journal publication through subscription sales, a model in which the reader (or the reader's library proxy) pays for access, many open-access publishers have shifted to article-processing charges, or APCs, as their primary revenue stream, a model in which the author (or the author's funder proxy) pays for distribution. Because many scientific journals had long required page fees for the production and reproduction of graphical elements, for instance, and because the grants that fund the vast majority of scientific research frequently covered those fees, the transition was relatively simple: publishing costs that enable researchers to make their results available to the world are now written into grants in the sciences. In fact, many granting agencies today require open-access distribution (whether through a "gold" publication or through a "green" repository) as a condition of funding.

In many other fields, however, not only is the available grant funding generally too low to accommodate the inclusion of significant publishing charges, but the vast majority of research is either nominally supported by the scholar's institution or is self-funded. In many cases, the author-pays model would literally mean that the author was paying, a significant new barrier to publication for many. Given that, we need to ask whether shifting the costs from reader-pays to author-pays opens up new inequities, shifting the disparities in access to research publications from the consumer side to the producer side of the equation. Researchers who are working in fields in which there is not significant grant funding available, or who are at institutions that cannot provide publishing subventions, might under such a model not be able to get their work into circulation in the same way as those in grant-rich fields or at well-heeled institutions. There are alternatives, of course, including "platinum" OA publications that do not require author fees but are instead funded through new collective-action models, such as the Open Library of the Humanities. If the goals behind enabling public access to scholarly publications include basic principles of equity in access to knowledge, we need to create more such models and to guard against the introduction of new barriers to participating in the production and dissemination of knowledge.

These are all real challenges, and it's important to acknowledge that a large-scale transition of scholarly communication to an emphasis on public access wouldn't be easy. It would, however, be an extraordinary form of generosity, and a powerful demonstration of the commitment of our institutions of higher education to the public good. Enabling access to scholarly work does not just serve the goal of undoing its commercialization or removing it from a market-driven, competition-based economy, but rather is a first step in facilitating public engagement with the knowledge that universities produce. Generous thinking requires us not to give up in the face of the seemingly insurmountable financial and institutional obstacles to open access and challenges us instead to start figuring out what it will take to get around them.

Public Engagement

The potential for such generous thinking stems from our willingness to engage the public with our work, a willingness that offers much to our advantage where it exists, but that cannot be taken for granted. If we publish our work in ways that enable any interested reader to access it, that work will be more read, more cited, and create more impact for us and for our fields. Admittedly, this so-called citation advantage has often been contested. Patrick Gaulé and Nicolas Maystre argue, for instance, that a self-selection mechanism is at work; their evidence suggests that authors of high-quality work are more likely to choose open-access venues, and thus their higher rate of citation is more attributable to the work's quality than to its accessibility. However, studies such as that done by Yassine Gargouri and colleagues suggest that open access nonetheless demonstrably increases citation rates independent of quality. (Steve Hitchcock, in fact, gathered a lengthy bibliography of studies, updated through 2013, of the effects of open access on citation impact.) And it stands to reason: making work more openly accessible enables scholars in areas of the world without extensive library budgets, as well as US-based instructors and students at undergraduate teaching institutions and secondary schools, to use it in their own work. Making work openly accessible also allows it to reach other interested readers in a wide range of careers who may not have access to research libraries. Expanding our readership in these ways would seem an unmitigated good.

Any yet, we must acknowledge the ways in which we resist opening our work to broader publics and the reasons for that resistance. Many of us keep our work confined within our own discourse communities because we fear the consequences of making it available to broader publics—and not without justification. There are times when (and topics on which) the general public seems determined to misunderstand us and to interpret what we say with focused hostility, and that hostility can pose real threats. Campaigns by groups that use watchlists to target faculty they see as indoctrinating students with "left-wing propaganda," such as Turning Point USA, endanger the livelihoods, and even the lives, of many scholars whose work explores race, gender, sexuality, and other areas of structural inequity. These campaigns are an extreme, but there are manifestations of much lower levels of hostility toward academic work in our culture that many of us experience every day, forms of resentment and dismissiveness that Tom Nichols associates with a general rejection of expertise in contemporary culture. And because the subject matter of much of the humanities and social sciences seems as though it should be accessible, our determination to wrestle with difficult questions and our use of expert methods and vocabularies can feel threatening to many readers. Admittedly, we at times deploy those methods and vocabularies as a defensive shield, developed to demonstrate our seriousness to those on campus who might find our fields too "soft" or to win points in some conflict within our own discipline. But that shield keeps many readers from engaging with our work fully. They fail to understand us; we take their failure to understand as an insult. (Sometimes it is, but not always.) Given this failure to communicate, we see no harm in keeping our work closed off from the public, arguing that we're only writing for a small group of specialists anyhow. So why would public access matter?

The problem, of course, is that the more we close our work away from the public, and the more we turn away from dialogue across the boundaries of the academy, the more we undermine the public's willingness to support our research and our institutions. As public humanities scholars including Kathleen Woodward have argued, the major crisis facing the funding of higher education is an increasingly widespread conviction that education is a private responsibility rather than a public good. We wind up strengthening that conviction and worsening the crisis when we treat our work as private, by keeping it amongst ourselves. Closing our work away from nonscholarly readers and keeping our conversations private might protect us from public criticism, but it cannot protect us from public apathy, a condition that may be far more dangerous in the current economic and political environment. This is not to say that working in public doesn't bear risks and require careful preparation for potential conflict, especially for scholars working in politically engaged fields, but it is to say that only through dialogue that moves outside our own discourse communities will we have any chance of convincing the broader public, including our governments, of the relevance of our work.

While increasing the availability of scholarly work online has the potential to make it more read, more cited, and more used by other scholars, expanding its potential to engage a public readership may require different kinds of openness, inviting those readers into discussions they might otherwise dismiss as "academic." Ensuring that we find ways to issue such invitations has potential benefits not just for the individual scholar but for the field in which she works. The more that well-researched, thoughtful scholarship on contemporary cultural issues is available to, for instance, journalists covering those issues for popular venues, the richer the discourse in those publications will become—increasing, not incidentally, the visibility of institutions of higher education and their importance for the culture at large.

Beyond the ability of openly distributed scholarship to foster this kind of public impact, however, is the fact that engaging readers in thoughtful discussions about the important issues we study lies at the core of the academic mission. It is at the heart of our values. We do not create knowledge in order to hoard it, but instead, every day, in the classroom, in the lecture hall, and in our writing, we embrace an ethic that I've come to think of as "giving it away." This idea comes to me from David Foster

Wallace's *Infinite Jest,* and its rendering of the ethos of Alcoholics Anonymous:

> Giving It Away is a cardinal Boston AA principle. The term's derived from an epigrammatic description of recovery in Boston AA: "You give it up to get it back to give it away." Sobriety in Boston is regarded as less a gift than a sort of cosmic loan. You can't pay the loan back, but you can pay it forward, by spreading the message that despite all appearances AA works, spreading this message to the next new guy who's tottered in to a meeting and is sitting in the back row unable to hold his cup of coffee. The only way to hang onto sobriety is to give it away. (344)

This requirement to pass on what one has learned has its origins in the program's twelfth step, in which the recovering alcoholic carries the message to others who need it. The sharing that this sense of "giving it away" invokes—the loan that can never be paid back, but only forward—includes that sharing done at meetings, telling one's own story, not as a means of self-expression but rather as an act of generosity that enables the addict to transcend the limitations of the self. "Giving it away" is thus a profoundly ethical mode of engaging with others in a community based around a common need. More than that, though, in *Infinite Jest* "giving it away" appears to be the only means of escaping the self-destructive spiral of addiction and self-absorption that constitutes not an anomalous state but rather the central mode of being in the contemporary United States.

This sense of "giving it away," of paying forward knowledge that one likewise received as a gift, functions well as a description of the best ethical practices of scholars and educators. We teach, as we were taught; we publish, as we learn from the publications of others. We cannot pay back those who came before us, but we can and do give to those who come after. Our participation in an ethical, voluntary scholarly community is grounded in the obligations we hold for one another, obligations that, as I discussed in chapter 1, cannot simply be discharged, precisely because they derive from the generosity we have received.

Like the stirring sense in the Budapest Open Access Initiative of "uniting humanity in a common intellectual conversation and quest for knowledge," this kind of idealism is all well and good, but it of course doesn't adequately account for an academic universe in which we are evaluated based on individual achievement and in which prestige often overrides all other values. I will explore the institutional responsibility for and effects of that bias toward prestige in the next chapter; here, I want to think a bit about its effects on the individual scholar, as well as that scholar's role in perpetuating this hierarchical status quo. Surveys conducted both by the research organization Ithaka S+R and by Diane Harley and the Center for Studies in Higher Education at UC Berkeley reach the same conclusion: "a fundamentally conservative set of faculty attitudes continues to impede systematic change" in our scholarly communication system (Schonfeld and Housewright 2). Scholars choose to publish in those venues that are perceived to have the highest influence on their peers, and given the ways that competition structures value in the scholarly marketplace, that influence is often imagined to increase with exclusivity. Barbara Fister suggests, in fact, that this form of exclusivity or prestige functions in the academic economy like a "weird sort of fake financial derivative," a second-order market in which we trade not on the quality of the work itself but on the attributed quality of its metadata (Untitled comment). The more difficult it is to get an article into a journal, the higher the perceived value of—and the rewards for—having done so. This reasoning makes a certain kind of sense, of course, and yet the prestige that it relies upon too easily shades over into a sense that the more exclusive a publication's audience, the higher its value. If we place our work where "just anyone" could see it, it seems, its value would be significantly diminished.

This is, at its most benign, a self-defeating attitude; if we privilege exclusivity above all else, we should not be surprised by the limited circulation that results. And whatever the prestige market might suggests, it is when our work fails to circulate that its value truly declines. As David Parry has commented, "Knowledge that is not public is not knowledge." It is only in giving that work away, in making it available to the publics around us, that we produce knowledge. Only in escaping the confines of our individual selves and sharing our thinking with others can we pay forward what we have been so generously given. Moreover, approaching our scholarship from this generous perspective requires less of a change than it might initially sound. As Peter Suber and the Budapest initiative noted in remarks quoted above, one of the key determinants in making open access possible is that most of the players in the scholarly communication chain have always been engaged in a process of "giving it away": authors, reviewers, scholarly editors, and others involved in the process have long offered their work to others without requiring direct compensation. The question is how we offer it, and to whom.

In fact, the entire system of scholarly communication runs on an engine of generosity, one that does not just evade but in its way confounds market principles. As I noted in the last chapter, Lewis Hyde's exploration of the logic of artistic production acknowledges art's simultaneous existence within the structures of the market and the gift economy, but finally concludes that "where there is no gift there is no art" (11). So too the work of scholarship, which exists both within the commodified world of publishing and within a realm of open exchange that demonstrates through its commitment to the collective the ways that private enterprise can never fully provide for the public good. So rather than consigning our work to the market economy, allowing it to be contained and controlled by corporate actors that profit at higher education's expense, might all of the members of the university community—researchers, instructors, libraries, presses, and administrations—instead work to develop and support a system of scholarly communication that highlights the strengths of the gift economy? What if, for instance, we understood sustainability in scholarly communication not as the ability to generate revenue, but instead as the ability to keep the engine of generosity running? What if we were to embrace scholarship's existence in the gift economy and make a gift of our work to the world?

In asking those not entirely rhetorical questions, I want to be certain to distinguish between this gift economy and the generous thinking that underwrites it, on the one hand, and on the other, the injunction to work for free produced by the devaluing of much intellectual and professional labor within the so-called information economy. A mode of forced volunteerism has spread perniciously throughout contemporary culture, compelling college students and recent graduates to take on exploitative unpaid internships in order to "get a foot in the door," forcing creative professionals to do free work in order to "create a portfolio," and so on. And of course there are too many academic equivalents: vastly underpaid adjunct instructors, overworked graduate assistants, an ever-growing list of mentoring and other service requirements that fall disproportionately on the shoulders of junior faculty, women faculty, and faculty of color. Turning professional positions in scholarly communication, such as the managing editor of a journal, into the kind of un- or under-funded service opportunities that mostly devolve onto early career scholars—perhaps especially where those positions are accompanied by the promise of some hypothetical future reward resulting from the experience—is not generosity; it's exploitation.

Labor, in fact, is the primary reason that I resist the notion that all scholarly publications can be made available for free online. While the scholarship itself might be provided without charge, many of its authors have been paid by their employers or their granting organizations and will be compensated with a publication credit, a line on a c.v., a positive annual review outcome. Reviewers are rarely paid (almost never by journals, very modestly by book publishers), but they receive insight into developing work and the ability to shape their fields and support their communities by way of compensation. There is, however, a vast range of other labor that is necessary for the production of publications, even when distributed online: submissions must be managed and tracked as they are sent out for review; authors must be communicated with; accepted articles must be copyedited and typeset or entered into content management systems and proofread; websites must be hosted and designed and promoted. And this labor too often remains invisible. As Martin Eve has pointed out, "The technological imagination that envisages such bright futures for scholarly communications is often not so good at recognizing the labour that would sit behind such possibilities" ("Open Publication" 33). And attempts to deprofessionalize this labor, to wave it off as doable by volunteers, places the entire enterprise at risk. Unless we recognize and appropriately compensate publishing as labor, unless we account for that labor in assessing the overall cost of publishing, the engine of scholarly communication may cease to function.

Where I am asking for generosity then—for giving it away—it is from those who are fully credited and compensated, those who can therefore afford to be generous: those tenured and tenure-track faculty and other fully employed members of our professions who can and should contribute to the world the products of the labor that they have already been supported in undertaking. Similarly, generosity is called for from those institutions that can and should underwrite the production of scholarship on behalf of the academy and the public at large. It is our mission, and our responsibility, to look beyond our own walls to the world beyond, to enlarge the gifts that we have received by passing them on to others. Those of us who can afford to support generous practices in scholarly communication must commit to making our work as publicly, openly available as possible, and we should commit to supporting and sustaining the not-for-profit organizations that work to help us do so. Doing so requires that we hold the potential for public engagement with our work among our highest values, that we understand such potential engagement as a public good that we can share in creating.

Public Intellectuals

Critics of open access often argue, as I noted earlier, that the public couldn't possibly be interested in scholarly work, not least because they couldn't possibly understand it, and that there is therefore no particular reason to ensure their access to it. Some critics go even further. Robin Osborne, for instance, argues that open access could *reduce* the accessibility of scholarly publications to the general reader, as publications that do not rely on subscriptions for their revenue stream "have no concern for satisfying subscribers or for the number of readers," and thus are less subject to the kinds of editorial intervention that make publications engaging to a broad readership (103). Running behind this conclusion is Osborne's rather extraordinary understanding of how the market for scholarly communication functions:

> By my choice of a highly specialist journal, generalist journal, university press or a popular publisher, in a magazine for sixth-formers or a political weekly, I signal to whom I think I have made my research accessible. Those who, on the basis of those signals, expect that they will understand and are interested enough in what I think and what I have said, pay for access to my thoughts. (102)

If this were, in fact, the case, there would seem little cause for alarm about the state of contemporary publishing: those who want it and can understand it are willing to pay for it and are supported by my thoughtfulness in tailoring my arguments to the audience at hand. But even leaving aside the question of the public's willingness to pay for access to ideas (about which a conversation with just about anyone in publishing today might begin to dissuade you), there are two key problems with this line of thinking that we must encounter: first, that the "audience" is not merely at hand, waiting for the delivery of my research results, but instead must be engaged, invited to care about the work. And second, that I am unlikely to have been anywhere near so thoughtful about my choice of publishing venue, or anywhere near so skillful in tailoring my communication practices to that venue, as this model implies.

The fact is that those critics who dismiss open access on the basis that the public cannot understand the work and so does not need access to it may be wrong in the conclusion, but they are not wrong in the premise; our work often does not communicate well to general readers. And that's fine, to an extent: communication within a discourse community plays a crucial role in that community's development, and thus there must always be room for expert-to-expert communication of a highly specialized nature. But we have privileged that inwardly focused sharing of work to the exclusion of more outwardly directed communication. Scholars are not rewarded—and in fact are at times actively derided—for publishing in popular venues. And because the values instantiated by our rewards systems have a profound effect on the ways we train our students, both directly and indirectly, we are building the wall between academic and public discourse higher and higher with every passing cohort. One key means of tearing down that wall, of thinking generously about the ways the university connects with the surrounding communities, would be for scholars to do more writing designed for public audiences.

There has been a strong push for this kind of public-facing writing among scientists and social scientists in recent years, and a number of scholars in the humanities have recently moved in this direction as well by developing public-facing publications that bring their ideas to greater public attention; one might see, for instance, the important work and significant impact of the *Los Angeles Review of Books* and *Public Books*. There are also a host of individual and group blogs that demonstrate the ways that many scholars are already working in multiple registers, engaging with multiple audiences. These venues open scholarly concerns and conversations to a broader readership and demonstrate the public value of academic approaches to understanding contemporary culture.

But these venues present some complications for the ways that we understand our work as scholars. If we are to open our ideas to larger public audiences, we need to give some serious thought to the ways we write, the mode and voice of our writing. There is, after all, something we should face up to in Bruce Cole's anti-intellectual dismissal of much scholarship in the humanities, which he claims is "alienating students and the public" with its "opacity, triviality, and irrelevance." I would personally dispute all three of those adjectives, but must acknowledge that the where the first exists, it creates the possibility of the second and third: because mainstream readers often do not understand our prose, they are able to assume (sometimes dismissively, and sometimes defensively) that the ideas it contains are overblown and insignificant. And it's important to add that this concern about academic writing isn't restricted to conservative critics. Editors at many mainstream publications have noted the difficulty in getting scholarly authors to address broader audiences in the ways their venues require. We have been trained to focus on complexity and nuance, to account for complications, to defuse disagreements in advance. The result is often lines of argumentation, and lines of prose, that are far from straight-forward. Getting past the accusations of triviality and irrelevance requires us to open up our rhetoric, to tell the story of our work in a manner that communicates to a generally educated reader how and why what we do matters.

This is not to say that all academic writing should be published in mainstream venues, or should necessarily be done in a public register. But I do believe that we would benefit from doing more work in ways that are not just technically but also rhetorically accessible to the public. And when I say "we," I mean as many of us as possible. Tom Nichols, in *The Death of Expertise,* argues for the need for greater communication between experts and the public, but suggests that such public communication might best be channeled through particular voices:

> To be honest, I suspect that most experts and scholars would probably prefer that laypeople avoid [reading their work], because they would not understand most of what they were reading and their attempt to follow the professional debate would likely produce more public confusion than enlightenment.
>
> This is where public intellectuals, the people who can bridge the gap between experts and laypeople, might shoulder more responsibility. (205)

I agree without question that public intellectuals should take on more responsibility for communicating scholarly work to public audiences—but I strongly believe that we are all, to varying extents, called to be public intellectuals. Our work in the classroom demonstrates that finding ways to explain difficult intellectual concepts and their expression to nonexpert readers, bringing those readers into our discussions and helping them make sense of the work going on in our fields, is already central to our profession. This movement across levels of expertise might enable greater connection with publics outside the classroom as well, helping to get them invested and involved in the work taking place on college and university campuses and thereby building support for that work. But for that project to be successful, scholars need to be prepared to bridge the communication gaps themselves, by honing our ability to alternate speaking with one another and speaking with different audiences.

In an early draft of this book, I'd described this process as one of *translating*, of seeking ways to communicate ideas to a public that might not speak the language in which they were originally conveyed. Sharon Leon, however, wisely pointed out a need for caution in the use of that term, which in some fields "has taken on a sheen of condescension toward the public," emphasizing the public's inability to understand. And in many fields such "translation" is not considered intellectual work, and does not count as such in their systems of evaluation; it's rather a secondary process associated with popularizing the actual work. Coming as I do from literary studies, I have a somewhat different view of the notion of translation, which has been crucial to making the intellectual and artistic production of one culture available to others. That translation remains undervalued, however, is clear; it is too often imagined to be an algebraic process of substitution whereby words in one language are replaced with words in another, with a kind of transparency as the goal. As translation theorists such as Lawrence Venuti make clear, however, the work of translation requires far more in the way of interpretation than we often recognize; the translator must face the loss of "resonances and allusions" in one language while building new connections for readers in another. Translation is thus itself a process of writing, and one that reaches across and connects multiple cultures. It's for that reason that the concept remains useful to me, though I understand Leon's concern. It's a concern shared by Steven Lubar, who in "Seven Rules for Public Humanists" points to the importance for public scholars of serving simultaneously as experts and as translators, noting that while translation may be important to the work of facilitating public involvement in scholarly projects, the concept too often suggests that we do the real work in one register and then later turn it into something else for the outside world. For Lubar, "The work of public engagement comes not after the scholarship, but as part of the scholarship." And that simultaneity may be the key: it's not that scholars need to learn to translate their work for more general audiences after the fact, but rather that we need to learn how to move fluidly between the highly specialized languages of our fields and the languages used outside them, to stretch across those languages and find the resonances and allusions that make our work engaging. We need, in other words, to learn a professional form of code switching.

"Code switching" as a term has its origin in linguistics and is used to explore how and why speakers move between multiple languages within individual speech instances. The concept was borrowed by scholars and teachers of rhetoric and composition as a means of thinking about students' need to move between vernacular and academic languages in addressing particular audiences at particular moments. Rebecca Moore Howard has noted that

> the linguistic principle behind the pedagogy of code-switching is that all language varieties are equally effective in their communities; that the standard variety prevails in the academic community as well as in the communities of American commerce; that students who wish to succeed in these communities must learn the standard; and that teachers should therefore encourage students of non-standard varieties to switch to the standard in the classroom. (266)

Inescapably, however, code switching in this pedagogical context is deeply racialized. The injunction to code-switch, as Vershawn Ashanti Young has argued, requires students to "recognize the superiority of standard English and the people associated with it"

(55), a requirement that enforces the need for black students and other students of color to maintain a DuBoisian double consciousness in order to belong. Howard argues that the effect of this injunction is "eradicationism" (274), effectively eliminating the languages of the marginalized in mainstream discourse. Young likewise argues that code switching in writing pedagogy is "a strategy to negotiate, side-step and ultimately accommodate bias against the working-class, women, and the ongoing racism against the language habits of blacks and other non-white peoples" by inculcating the dominance of standard English (51).

My use of the notion of code switching in the present context is thus challenging; code switching as a hegemonic pedagogical tool requires displacing a lived vernacular with a dominant variant. The command to code switch in an unequal environment is inevitably a tool of power. But so, I want to argue, is scholars' assumption that academic English as we perform it is the "standard variety"; in fact, it is as much a lived vernacular as any, but a vernacular based in privilege. Given that privilege, our refusal to code switch, insisting that only our language will serve to explain our ideas, is not an act of resistance. We can and should speak that expert language with one another, but if it is the only language we speak, we exclude the possibility of allying ourselves with other communities. Christopher Long argues, in fact, from the perspective of the field of philosophy, that the anti-intellectualism that scholars find rampant within contemporary American culture is "reinforced by academic professionalism," which results in the further alienation of the public from the academy (2); our insistence on a professional language may not just keep us from being broadly understood, but in fact exacerbate the hostility we perceive around us.

None of what I am suggesting here is simple; we cannot merely adopt a common language that will make us understood and our work beloved by all. Nor should we abandon the precise academic languages that undergird the rigor of the writing we share with one another. But it is nonetheless worth asking how judicious code switching, as a means of acknowledging the effects of our educational and professional privilege and inviting others into our discussions, could become a more regular part of our scholarly work. Might more scholars, for instance, develop pieces of writing designed for and in communication with public audiences that open up our more internally focused arguments? This mode of public-facing writing—as many editors of mainstream intellectual publications would note—is very different from scholars' usual mode of professional writing, and by and large it is not something we are trained to do. A number of recent programs present opportunities for such training; these include the seminars conducted by the OpEd Project, which seek to increase the diversity of voices represented in major publications, as well as a series of workshops sponsored by the National Endowment for the Humanities and coordinated by the editors of the Object Lessons book series, which focus on helping "scholars and nonfiction authors write for broader audiences while maintaining intellectual rigor and developing their academic profiles" ("Apply to an Object Lessons Workshop"). Workshops such as these can help scholarly authors focus and express the significance of their ideas in ways that help broader audiences engage with them. Many, many more such workshops are needed—and, in fact, this kind of writing instruction (including other practical genres of writing such as the grant proposal) should ideally become part of graduate training across the university.

There has been, perhaps unsurprisingly, a great deal of recent debate about the value of the public intellectual and the role that scholars might play in the development of a healthier public discourse. Mark Greif, for instance, in asking what's wrong with today's public intellectuals, expresses dismay about the degree to which scholars seem to resist that role:

> A large pool of disgruntled free-thinking people who are not actually starving, gathered in many local physical centers, whose vocation leads them to amass an enormous quantity of knowledge and skill in disputation, and who possess 24-hour access to research libraries, might be the most publicly argumentative the world has known.

Might be, except that too many of us shy away from taking our debates public, instead arguing with and for one another rather than rather than using our arguments to effect a public good. Benjamin Wurgaft is similarly skeptical about the public intellectual's potential, though less because of the inward-facingness of scholars and intellectuals than because of a more fundamental disjunction between the "public" and the "intellectual" in contemporary culture: "In the face of the widespread rejection of informed or expert opinion," Wurgaft asks, "can thinkers who address the public, not only remind us of the existence of trained and experienced judgment, but give us a feeling for its connection to our mundane lives?" Public intellectuals, in other words, face the challenge of demonstrating that their arguments have some bearing on the lived experience of their readers. But Wurgaft goes on to note that his concern has less to do with "the actions of specific thinkers and writers" than with "the condition of culture." Which is to say that, in order to evoke a sense of connection in their readers, writers need to understand the increasingly complex, multifarious nature of what we think of as the "public" today.

The relationship that scholarly authors bear toward the public good is in this view riven by uncertainty about who the public is, what the good might be, and what role the intellectual might play in creating and sustaining both. This is not a new problem; the condition of culture is and has always been characterized by divisions and exclusions, making it impossible for any writer to address the idealized singularity of the Habermasian public sphere and instead allowing only for access to a subset of Nancy Fraser's "plurality of competing counterpublics" (61). It's important, however, to examine the possibility that scholars' retreat from engagement with the public—however mythical that unified body has always been—might be a contributing factor to the public's fragmentation. As Alan Jacobs has noted in considering the withdrawal of Christian intellectuals from public engagement, "Subaltern counterpublics are essential for those who have never had seats at the table of power, but they can also be immensely appealing to those who feel that their public presence and authority have waned" ("The Watchmen"). The similar withdrawal of scholars into private discourse has produced a tighter sense of connection and the comfort of being understood, but at the cost of creating an intellectual gated community, removing scholarly issues and perspectives from public view, and removing the potential for using those issues to build alliances and create solidarity among counterpublics. Christopher Long, in fact, argues that public forms of social inquiry, conducted collaboratively by thinkers on and off campus, are a necessary means through which an otherwise amorphous, inchoate public might become the articulated public that John Dewey saw as necessary to the creation of a genuinely democratic society. And Corey Robin likewise argues that the public does not precede the intellectual, like an audience simply waiting for entertainment or instruction; rather, the public intellectual is for Robin "the literary equivalent of the epic political actor, who sees her writing as a transformative mode of action, a thought-deed in the world." The transformation that Robin's public intellectual seeks is, not least, the creation of the public itself, activating that public for further action on its own behalf.

If we are to heed Jacobs's and Long's call for a return to public discourse, Greif's sense of the possibilities for that discourse, Wurgaft's skepticism about our ability to connect with the public, and Robin's recognition that our role requires us to help create that public in the first place, we'll have to contend with the public's multiplicity. We can only ever speak, at any given moment, with subsets of the public, and this, Jacobs notes, inevitably becomes a problem of writing:

> I have felt for my entire career the difficulties of deciding where to speak and how. About a decade into my professional life it suddenly dawned on me that, unlike the people I went to graduate school with and the professors I saw as my mentors and models, I was never going to have a single audience. It would be necessary for me at times to speak to the church; at other times to believers from other religious traditions; at other times to my fellow academics; and at yet other times to the American public at large. This meant that I would not be able to formulate a single writerly voice, a single mode of articulation, a single rhetoric that I could deploy in any and all situations. ("The Watchmen")

The publics we seek connection with may be different from those with whom Jacobs speaks, and they're likely different from those publics sought by our colleagues. The key is to ask ourselves with whom we want to be in dialogue, and most importantly why, so that we can begin to understand ourselves as participants not just in those conversations but in those publics.

We'll also need to think carefully about the best means and venues for conversations with the publics we hope to bring together. As André de Avillez and his colleagues note in exploring the possibilities for public philosophy, spaces for public discussion are often not readily found:

> Even if scholars wish to participate in public philosophy, there remains a noticeable shortage of venues (be they local or online) where members of the public may gather and form communities around the practice of philosophical inquiry: venues where the public use of reason is promoted and where the specialist will not only share research with the public, but will engage lay readers in conversation, become attentive to the community's own inquiries, and ultimately collaborate with the community as it continues its inquiry. (137)

These are the spaces in which a public, in dialogue with scholarly modes of thought, might begin to articulate itself, as well as spaces in which scholars might begin to better understand the publics with which they are in dialogue. De Avillez and colleagues note the possibility that public intellectual blogs and other online discussion spaces present for such articulation, but they also point to the real difficulty of maintaining productive discussion online, given the omnipresence of trolls and other bad actors, and make clear "the assiduous effort required to cultivate and maintain collegiality in the community" (137). The best venue for public engagement, in other words, is not one that we might simply avail ourselves of—submit our work for publication, rent out for an evening—but is one that we must build, and maintain.

And all of that work of community building—imagining the publics we want to be part of, developing and maintaining the best means of supporting their organization—needs to recognized not just as a form of generous thinking, but as work. Scholars must do a much better job of supporting members of their own academic communities who work in public modes by understanding that their work is not just public, but also intellectual. Conventional academic modes of evaluation and assessment such as are used on many campuses are built on a tripartite division among research, teaching, and service, and too often—especially on campuses with a significant research mandate—things that don't meet a relatively narrow set of criteria for what gets considered "research" are filed away as "service," a distant third in priority. (That this is less true of regional comprehensive institutions, liberal-arts colleges, and community colleges, where teaching and outreach are not subordinated to—indeed, often not separated from—research, is important to consider in the context of the ways that institutions are ranked and hierarchized, on the one hand, and the ways that the public attributes value to them, on the other. I'll take this up in more detail in the next chapter.) As a result, work that does not hew as closely as possible to the dominant form in which scholarship is done is often undervalued or even actively dismissed back on campus. Public exhibitions, online interactive projects, community discussions: too often, these forms of public work are granted far less weight and importance than a peer-reviewed scholarly article. And even when the public-facing work takes the form of published writing, it is often assumed to be less developed, less authoritative, less important, since it probably has not been through academic processes of peer review. In fact, writing in mainstream publications is likely to have been far more stringently edited than that in most scholarly journals, since editors for mainstream publications often work much more closely with writers and their prose than academic editors. This editing process can hone an idea in important ways, clarifying it for both writer and reader. But clarity is too often mistaken for simplicity. Presenting an argument or issue in a straightforward fashion runs the risk of inviting not just debate but dismissal. And worse yet, the academic universe too often assumes that a scholar who writes for a public market must "dumb down" key ideas in order to do so.

As Mark Greif has pointed out, this assumption affects not only the ways that public intellectual work is evaluated by the academy but also the work that academics want to present to the public. In his experience editing *n+1*, he received submissions from many brilliant writers who

> merrily left difficulty at home, leapt into colloquial language with both feet, added unnatural (and frankly unfunny) jokes, talked about TV, took on a tone chummy and unctuous. They dumbed down, in short—even with the most innocent intentions. The public, even the "general reader," seemed to mean someone less adept, ingenious, and critical than themselves.

This seems to run counter to the argument I made earlier in this section, that academic writers need to learn some mode of code-switching in order to enter into dialogue with broader publics, but in fact it cuts to the heart of the problem: we too often do not know how to speak with those publics, because we do not understand them. We forget that many members of those publics have studied the same fields we have—that, as Martin Eve reminded me in the public discussion of this book's draft, many members of those publics were once our students, and so have been taught *by us* to engage in serious intellectual debate. And, as chapter 1 suggests, we too often do not understand these publics because we do not genuinely listen to them, and particularly to those publics with which we disagree, with often disastrous effects.

If scholars are to engage as public intellectuals, then, we need to make room for the public in our arguments, in our projects, and in our prose. But we also need to understand that our arguments, projects, prose are merely one part of a much larger, multivoiced conversation. And this is key: Having found a way to connect with a broader audience, having recognized that part of our work is supporting that audience in its articulation into a public, how do we then best help to facilitate the activation of that public to work on its own behalf?

Public Scholarship

Here is where our working in public—creating public access, valuing public engagement, becoming public intellectuals— transforms into the creation of a genuinely public scholarship, a generous scholarship, relying on a diverse set of practices that are not simply performed for the public but that include and are in fact given over to the publics with whom we work. In public scholarship, members of our chosen communities enter into our projects not just as readers but as participants, as stakeholders, and as partners. Public scholarship allows the venues for engaging with those communities to expand beyond the monograph or the journal article to include a range of forms in which the publics with whom we work can engage directly with the materials of our fields. After all, when de Avillez and colleagues note the shortage of venues in which public thought and deliberation can take place, they mean *publications,* and in that respect, they are correct. But if we broaden our sense of the spaces in which scholarly thought can take place to include museum and gallery exhibitions, interactive web archives, and a range of other projects designed to support and facilitate the exploration and interpretation of all participants—including community-oriented publication models such as that being developed by the *Public Philosophy Journal*—then the number of potential venues grows, as do the possibilities for connection. This growth might allow our thinking to escape the procrustean bed of our traditional publication formats and instead take the shape best suited to its purposes of engagement, over and above those of argument.

Public participation in scholarly discovery is often difficult for scholars to imagine, but recent experiments in what's been called "citizen science" provide some potentially interesting examples. These are projects, such as Galaxy Zoo, that go beyond crowdsourcing by enlisting networked participants not just in mass repetitive tasks but in the actual process of discovery. Galaxy Zoo, which launched in 2007, initially invited interested volunteers to assist with classifying the hundreds of thousands of galaxies contained in a sample from the Sloan Digital Sky Survey. They did that, far faster and more thoroughly than any lab full of grad students and post-docs could have. But those volunteers have also become active participants in significant discoveries that have resulted in dozens of published papers over the last decade. These papers include studies of the project itself, which indicate that volunteers are motivated to participate by their interest in astronomy, their desire to contribute to research, their hope to learn more about science, and the fun they have in the process (Raddick et al.).

If this is one form that citizen science takes, what might the citizen humanities or social sciences look like? It might look like museum exhibits such as *Pacific Worlds* at the Oakland Museum of California, which engaged members of local Pacific communities in the planning and development processes, with the result that "what you see in our galleries includes not only the input of curators and historians, but of people that are featured speaking for themselves" (Fischer). It might look like *The September 11 Digital Archive*, developed by the American Social History Project and the Roy Rosenzweig Center for History and New Media at George Mason University, which presents first-hand accounts of the events of that day, along with photos, emails, and other archival materials from more than 150,000 participants, with the goal of "providing historical context for understanding those events and their consequences" by "allowing people to tell their stories, making those stories available to a wide audience." It might look like the New York Public Library Labs's *What's on the Menu?*, in which participants were invited to help transcribe, review, and geotag the library's massive digitized collection of historic menus, making them accessible for research and "opening the door to new kinds of discoveries." It might look like the *Baltimore Stories* project coordinated by the Dresher Center for the Humanities at the University of Maryland, Baltimore County, which used humanities scholarship as a convening force to bring community organizers, educators, and nonprofit organizations together with the university in order to "help frame and contextualize narratives of race in American cities" ("The Dresher Center"). It might look like the Organization for Transformative Works, a nonprofit activist organization that brings academic and public popular culture fans together in supporting a web archive that hosts a wide range of fan production, a journal that explores fan cultures and practices, and a range of other forms of advocacy for the creative and critical production of fans ("About the OTW").

What these projects have in common is that the cultural concern each of them explores is of compelling interest to the public that the project engages, precisely because that concern belongs to them. The work involved is theirs not just to learn from but to shape and define as well. As the Organization for Transformative Works notes in its values statement, the network is defined by a "volunteer-based infrastructure" and a "fannish gift economy," making clear that the organization is not just for the fans, but fully owned by the fans; the community comes first, in all its complex diversity, before the projects that it undertakes ("What We Believe"). This is a crucial aspect, as Steven Lubar reminds us, of public scholarship. Engaging publics in working with scholars to interpret, understand, preserve, and teach their cultures and histories—work of engagement that must be integrally part of the scholarship—has the potential to connect those publics with the university in ways that can create a vital new sense of belonging, but the university must be ready to understand itself as fully connected and in service to the broader community. I'll dig further into that requirement in the next chapter.

For the moment, however, I want to think a bit about ways that scholars might see the publics that they seek to engage. The relationship involved in the projects I describe above is not just a matter of "crowd-sourcing," as the involvement of active public participation in scholarly work is sometimes described. Crowd-sourcing has something of a mixed reputation, in fact. On the positive side, engaging a distributed set of participants in the work of research—whether identifying galaxies, transcribing and geo-tagging menu items, or enriching our understanding of climate history by "finding and recording historical weather observations in ships' logs" as in the *Old Weather* project (Blaser 50)—can speed the discovery process and bring a much broader range of perspectives to bear on the material under study by activating public curiosity. However, as the authors collected in the volume *Crowdsourcing Our Cultural Heritage* (edited by Mia Ridge) demonstrate, projects that seek such active participation must be fully open to the interests of those who participate; as the *Old Weather* project leads discovered, many of the volunteers who were transcribing the ships' logs began developing data sets that tracked their own interests, thus lending the project not just to tracing historical weather patterns but also phenomena such as the spread of the 1918 Spanish Flu (Blaser 53). A willingness to incorporate and pursue such participant discoveries, as Lucinda Blaser and other researchers who have developed successful community-engaged projects reiterate, is key to the project's success.

This participant focus is also crucial to ensuring that the publics engaged through crowd-sourcing are not treated as if they were a mere extension of the computerized system that coordinates their labor, as if the "mechanical Turk" metaphor used by Amazon in establishing its crowd-sourcing platform were literal. As a 2016 report from the Pew Research Center demonstrates, "online outsourcing" of research labor runs the risk of exploitation, as projects benefit from the uncredited appropriation of participants' creative labor and inadvertently contribute to the spread of the so-called gig economy (Hitlin). At the same time, however, the participant focus of genuinely community-engaged scholarship does not mean simply handing over the project to the interests of the crowd. As John Kuo Wei Tchen notes in his exploration of the founding of the "dialogic" Chinatown History Museum, such "ultrademocratic" tendencies, while laudable, disclaim scholars' responsibilities for their own participation. It's not incidental, after all, that the negative side of crowd-sourcing's reputation derives not just from this potential for abuse but also from the potential for misinformation that can arise from the unruly masses. Tom Nichols, for instance, argues in his defense of the role of the expert in contemporary culture that the assumption that "the Internet can serve as a way of crowd-sourcing knowledge conflates the perfectly reasonable idea of what the writer James Surowiecki has called 'the wisdom of the crowds' with the completely unreasonable idea that the crowds are wise because each member of the mob is also wise" (122). This is to say that groups require mechanisms for self-correction in order to manifest and elevate the wisdom they contain. Wikipedia, for instance, operates under a strict set of rules for the review of contributions and changes to the project. Critics have pointed out the many flaws in those rules—the degree to which, for instance, they permit certain kinds of systemic bias to flourish and allow editors with an axe to grind to control the direction of their areas of the project ("Criticism")—and the problems to which they lead are significant.

But these problems are not inevitable. This is perhaps where the self-reflexivity of humanities and social science-based critique, coupled with the generosity that is at the root of our thinking, might point the way toward better, more generative practices. Tchen points to the importance of ongoing dialogue in community-oriented work, noting that "the authorship of an exhibition, and therefore the authority associated with authorship, should be viewed as a shared and collaborative process and not as an either/or proposition" (297). That shared and collaborative process must extend to an ongoing discussion and review of the editorial and other principles under which community-based projects operate, enabling public scholarship to develop and maintain structures that are not just self-regulating but also self-critical. As my colleague Avi Santo and I argued in a white paper on open peer review practices in humanities scholarship, successful processes based in communities of practice require carefully developed guidelines that foster the kinds of engagement we seek— and those guidelines, and the community's functioning within them, must be equally subject to community review as is the work itself. The understandings that guide scholars' engagement with broader publics require the same guidance and the same commitment to ongoing review.

Open peer review has of course met with resistance to the notion that members of the public can serve as "peers." It is, however, worth considering the ways that the academy might benefit from a shift away from an understanding of the "peer" as a "credentialed colleague" and toward the recognition that "peer status might only emerge through participation" in the processes of a community of practice (Fitzpatrick and Santo 8). Sheila Brennan, in the online discussion of the draft of this chapter, pointed out the admirable practices of the National Postal Museum in bringing together scholars and collectors in their annual symposium and publications, as well as in thinking through their collections and exhibits, which has led to a broadened sense of engagement with and ownership of the museum's work; this kind of engagement requires those with different forms of expertise to recognize one another as potential peers. The importance of that recognition should not be underestimated: the way we define the notion of the peer has profound consequences not just for determining whom we consider under that label but also who considers themselves to be a part of that category. As I noted in the introduction, Kelly Susan Bradbury has similarly explored this issue with respect to the term "intellectual," pointing out the ways that, for instance, traditional academic exclusions of the more applied interests of adult education programs from that category results in those who participate in such programs rejecting the notion of the intellectual as part of their self-definition. This rejection inevitably exacerbates tendencies and beliefs in American culture that we perceive as anti-intellectual. Opening the notion of the intellectual, or the peer, to a much broader range of forms of critical inquiry and active project participation has the potential to reshape relations between town and gown, to lay the groundwork for more productive conversations across the borders of the campus, and to create an understanding of the extent to which the work of the academy matters for our culture as a whole.

If the purpose of public scholarship lies in helping members of the public undertake their own projects and assisting them in understanding and executing their roles as authors and interpreters, as Ronald Grele argued of public history as far back as 1981, scholars require an entirely different relationship both to their work and to the communities within which it is embedded. But what would happen if we were to open up not just our understandings of the terms through which we describe intellectual or scholarly work today, and not just our practices in engaging in that work, but the very institutions in which we spend our work lives? What would be required in order to transform our colleges and universities into places where this public-oriented, generous thinking can flourish? This kind of openness was one of the goals in the original establishment of the public land-grant colleges and universities under the Morrill Act, which authorized and supported those institutions in bringing crucial knowledge to the people of their states. That mission has often been met through extension programs that provide continuing education and outreach to state residents, often in practical areas such as agriculture and engineering. But it is crucial today that we think about what an extension program embracing the entire university, including the humanities and social sciences, might look like, and the ways that public universities might play a key role in bringing not just technical knowledge to the public but the liberal arts as well: not just tools for production, but tools for living. If the university is to win back public support, it must be prepared— structurally, strategically, at the heart of not just its mission statement but its actual mission—to place public service at the top of its priorities. What that might look like, and what that might require, is our focus ahead.

4

The University

American higher education is dominated by a model in which status is attained through the maintenance of scarcity, and academic elitism has become a defensive posture and abdication of implicit responsibility.
—MICHAEL M. CROW AND WILLIAM B. DABARS, *DESIGNING THE NEW AMERICAN UNIVERSITY*

This is not a problem for technological innovation or a market product. This requires politics.
—TRESSIE MCMILLAN COTTOM, *LOWER ED*

Roughly around the time that I first began sketching the outline for this book, I attended a day-long workshop on new models for university press publishing, for which the provost of a large state research university had been invited to give a keynote address. The talk came during a day of intensive discussions amongst the workshop's participants and university press and university library leaders, all of whom had a real stake in the future of the institution's role in disseminating scholarly work as openly as possible. And the keynote was quite powerful: the provost described his campus's efforts to embrace a renewed mission of public service, and he emphasized the role that broad public access to the faculty's work might play in transforming the environment in which the university operates today. The university's singular purpose is the public good, he said, but we are seen as being self-interested. Can opening our work up to the world help change the public discourse about us?

It was an inspiring talk, both rich in its analysis of how the university found its way into the economic and social problems it now faces and hopeful in thinking about new possibilities for renewed public commitment. Or, I should say, it was inspiring right up until the moment when the relationship between scholarly publishing and tenure and promotion was raised. And then it was as though someone had dimmed the lights: we heard about the importance of maintaining prestige within the faculty through modes of assessment that ensure that faculty members are publishing in the highest-quality venues, conventionally understood. Frustrated by that shift, I asked the provost during the question-and-answer period what the possibilities might be for a very important, highly visible research university that understands its primary mission to be service to the public good to remove the tenure and promotion logjam in the transformation of scholarly communication by convening the entire academic campus, from the provost through the deans, chairs, and faculty, in a collective project of revising—really, reimagining—all of its personnel processes and the standards on which they rely in light of a primary emphasis on the public good? What would become possible if all of those policies worked to ensure that what was considered excellence in research and teaching had its basis in the university's core service mission?

The provost's response was, more or less, that any institution that took on such a project would immediately lose competitiveness within its institutional cohort.

To say that this response was disappointing would be an understatement, but it was if nothing else honest. It made absolutely clear where, for most research universities, the rubber meets the road, and why lots of talk about openness, impact, public service, and generosity falls apart at the point at which it crosses paths with the more entrenched if unspoken principles around which our institutions are actually arranged today. The inability of institutions of higher education to transform their internal structures and processes in order to fully align with their stated mission and values may mean that the institutions have not in fact fully embraced that mission or those values. Or perhaps it's that there is a shadow mission—chasing Harvard—and a shadow value—competition—that exclude the possibility of that full alignment.

The worst part of it, if I am going to be honest, and the single fact that the chapter ahead is most driven by, is that *the provost was correct.* As currently structured, the entire system of higher education is engineered—from individual institutions to accrediting agencies, funding bodies, and the higher education press—to promote a certain kind of competitiveness that relies on a certain kind of prestige. Any institution that seeks to transform the rules or the goals of the competition without dramatically altering its relationship to the system as a whole is likely to suffer for it. In fact, in the actually existing world in which we live, our institutions are locked into constant competition with one another, as are pretty much all other aspects of contemporary American society. They compete for funding, for donors, for faculty, for students, for rankings, for attention. But that approach to institutional existence—what Christopher Newfield sums up as the mandate to "compete all the time"—forecloses a whole range of opportunities for our institutions, making it impossible for them to take any other approach (144). It leads, as numerous higher education researchers have explored at length, to an academic enterprise that defines itself based not on those whom it gathers in, but on the masses that it excludes. Andrew Delbanco goes on to note that "the quest for prestige is nothing new, but it has lately reached such frantic intensity that it is having seriously negative effects on the educational mission of many institutions" (117). Prestige, that which drives an institution to compete, that which renders it competitive, in fact undermines its mission, especially where that mission is or ought to be focused on public service. Prestige requires an institution to serve fewer rather than more; prestige is based not on how well those admitted are served but instead on how many are turned away. This peculiar prestige-by-exclusion operates at many levels in higher education: the prestige of publications, for instance, is in large part determined by their rejection rates. And focusing on prestige within the faculty creates a mode of invidious comparison that profoundly affects faculty members' attitudes toward and commitments to their institutions, resulting in a form of disgruntlement that a colleague of mine describes as "If There Were Any Justice, I'd Be at Princeton." These comparisons and exclusions work together to create an environment in which the university's benefits are understood to be best restricted to a small audience rather than shared with the world, which is overwhelmingly unworthy.

But as François Lachance reminds me, the word "prestige" has its roots in illusion, in a conjuring trick (Untitled comment on "Paradigm Shift"). Prestige is what convinces an audience that they've seen—that you've *done*—something impossible. Prestige draws that audience in, but only through deception. If the university's value in the public imagination—or, for that matter, in its own imagination—is built on prestige, we run the risk of having the illusion revealed as such. In fact, it *is* being revealed: small colleges and universities are closing, and larger ones are shutting down many of the areas of study that have long formed the core of higher education. And many, many of the ugly secrets of the university's operations are being made public.

I should note a few things before moving on. I began drafting this chapter shortly after reentering university life myself, after having spent six years as a member of the senior staff of a large scholarly society. It's possible that the time away allowed me to see institutional structures with fresh eyes, freeing me from the assumption that things simply are the way they are in some unchangeable sense and permitting a broader view of the possibilities. It's also possible, however, that my move back into campus life has further transformed my vision, though it's probably too soon to say whether things are clearer or more occluded. In a later section of this chapter I discuss some possibilities for rethinking the nature of the university as and in relation to community, and in the process I draw on a few programs from my own institution. No doubt my original interest in the opportunities presented by these programs was driven by the sunny optimism of the new arrival, in love with everything around her. Even then, however, there was intentionality behind that interest, as these programs and possibilities were key to my decision to join this particular institution.

But it's important to acknowledge that there's been no small amount of heartbreak, and even rage, involved in my relationship to this institution as well. I joined the faculty of Michigan State University in the fall of 2017, utterly infatuated by the institution's historic commitment to the public good, and I got to watch close-up as the shallowness of the contemporary commitment to that mission was exposed on the national and even international stage.

The failures here—which I'll discuss a bit later—are particularly spectacular; they have destroyed much of the public trust in the university, and they have touched off a campus-wide self-examination and mobilization to transform the university, its administration, and its structures from the ground up. How this will all turn out—what good the campus's fury might in the end be put to—remains to be seen. But all of us connected to the institution, both on campus and off, have been forced to contend with the extent to which the university—MSU, certainly, but far from alone—constantly undermines its relationship with the public through its failures to uphold the principles under which it claims to operate. And I have found myself, somewhat perversely perhaps, inspired by the rage and despair so evident in my colleagues and my students, because it's only that level of care on the part of the community that might present a chance to rebuild the university, requiring it to become an institution that actually lives out the values that it professes to uphold.

Back, however, to my exchange with that provost, about the possibilities for genuinely aligning university policies with the institution's primary mission of public service, possibilities that I recognize open a massive can of very wormy questions—wormy because it's clear that these are things that need to happen in order to make real change within institutions of higher education, and yet they generate significant anxiety about their consequences. What would happen, for instance, if the university were to let go of the notion of prestige and of the competition that creates it in order to better align its personnel and other processes with its deepest values? Could those institutions begin, individually and collectively, by rejecting the absurdly metrics-focused line they've been cudgeled into by the accrediting bodies that oversee them? How might we begin to rethink our institutions if we recognized that competition never really results in distinctive research and educational enterprises, but rather variations on a more thorough-going sameness, insofar as we're all chasing the same model? Is it possible for our institutions to accept that even when we seem to be trying to single ourselves out for support from the same funders or attendance from the same students, the competition that we have been drawn into has both fictional premises and fictional ends? What might become possible if we were able to decide that the real competition is not among institutions of higher education but rather between a vision of higher education as a public good and an understanding of higher education as a private responsibility? And what new goals could we set if, in seeking a collective grounding in a renewed commitment to higher education as a public good, we were able to recognize that, far more than our institutions need to differentiate themselves from one another, climbing over one another in some academic restaging of the Hunger Games, they need instead to collaborate, to build collectively the systems and capacities that all institutions of higher education need in order for the entire sector to thrive?

This chapter, happily, is not delving into the economics of the university; terrific work in that area has already been done, including Newfield's exploration of the damage wrought on the public university by insistent privatization, as well as Michael Fabricant and Stephen Brier's and Tressie McMillan Cottom's examinations of the relationship between the evolution of the university and the new economy. Rather, this chapter is focused on thinking through some other institutional possibilities, including emerging ways of returning to the mission of generosity at the heart of our institutions of higher education. In order to create the ground for these possibilities, we must collectively find ways to focus our institutions' attention, in the words of Michael Crow and William

Dabars, less on what we *can* think about and more on what we *need* to think about (207). One of the key things that we need to think about is the relationship between the structures and policies of our institutions of higher education and their mission of serving the public good, as well as about our roles—all of our roles—in effecting the organizational change required to ensure that such a relationship is paramount.

Public and Private Goods

There are, admittedly, massive differences within the category of "universities" that my argument in this chapter doesn't fully contend with. I am, to begin with, focused primarily on higher education in the United States, though much of what I describe is becoming sadly applicable in other parts of the world as well. I am also exclusively focused on not-for-profit higher education; one might see McMillan Cottom's *Lower Ed* for a powerful analysis of the basis and functioning of the for-profit sector as well as its profound differences in mission and orientation from the traditional institutions to which I attend here. Moreover, I am primarily focused on public institutions, which bear a particular responsibility and a particular history in this country, having been founded for the express purpose of providing higher education to the citizens of their states. Not only should upholding that mission form a core part of these institutions' identities, but it is these institutions that have lost the most, and that still stand the most to lose, from the deterioration of the relationship between the university and the general public. That said, the distinctions between publics and privates are diminishing thanks to radical shifts in the funding and admissions models under which those institutions operate, a circumstance that is largely the subject of

Newfield's *The Great Mistake*. And the need to build better relationships between the university and the broader public is an issue not just for public colleges and universities (though of course
it is a primary one for them) but also for those private institutions
that understand themselves to exist to whatever extent in the public service, insofar as those institutions rely on federal financial
aid, on public research funding, and on the good will of their
communities and the publics beyond. If today's universities are
to build successful relationships with those publics—if they are
to be understood as genuinely providing a public good—we must
not only argue for but also model what understanding our work
as a public good means.

This should probably begin with a bit of discussion of what
the public good *is* in the first place. As I noted in chapter 1, the
very notion of the public good is one of the concepts on which
the political Left and Right have been speaking past one another
in recent years: while most liberal and progressive voters would
today understand the public good as just what its name suggests—a
good that is held in common and shared by all, whose maintenance benefits everyone and therefore to which everyone must
contribute as they can—many conservative and libertarian voters
find the very declaration of the public good, much less the costs
of its upkeep, to be an imposition on their individual liberty. In
economic terms, a public good is nonexcludable and nonrivalrous, meaning that no one can be prevented from using it and
that no one's use reduces its availability for use by others. The
most common examples of such public goods include clean air
and water, from which everyone benefits. Others include public
services such as roads and firefighters. By contrast, private goods
are both excludable and rivalrous; they can be restricted for use
by paying customers, and their consumption by one customer can

diminish its availability to another. These private goods are market-based products, typically produced and distributed for profit. Goods that are nonexcludable but rivalrous are often described as common resources: it is these goods to which the "tragedy of the commons"—the overuse of shared natural resources—can apply. And, finally, there are club goods, goods that are excludable but nonrivalrous, restricted to paying customers but not diminished by any one customer's use.

The question, then, is what kind of good higher education, and the knowledge that it provides and creates, is and should be. Knowledge is certainly nonrivalrous; my possession of it should not preclude your ability to possess it as well. But where that knowledge and the higher education that fosters it might once have been imagined to be nonexcludable, available to anyone desiring it, it has since the middle of the twentieth century increasingly become excludable, restricted to those who can pay for it. Access to knowledge is today a club good, in other words, rather than the public good that was once imagined to best serve our society: nonexcludable and nonrivalrous, supported by all for the benefit of all. Over the last four decades, the culture of the United States has moved away from the understanding that educating children and young adults provides a benefit to society as a whole, and thus from the conviction that providing everyone with access to a high-quality education is a social responsibility and that no one should be excluded from that benefit. Instead, over that period, the pervasive assumption that parents should provide their children with the best education they can afford has taken root, with the result that education has come to be seen as a private responsibility, one best financed by individuals. Asking me to pay for your children's education is thought to be an undue imposition on my personal well-being; I am paying for my entrance to the club, and you should pay for your own. And, in fact, parts of the American educational system have been converted into private goods, not only restricted to those who can pay but limited to a certain number or type of participants. As a result of this privatization, education has come to be seen as rivalrous: if your child gets into the "good" school, there's one less seat available for my child. And even worse, it's coming to be understood as excludable in another sense beyond being restricted to those who pay for it, as arguments circulate that maybe education—especially higher education—isn't for everyone, and so maybe it's not a problem if some people don't have access.

Perhaps knowledge, and the educational systems that provide it, are not naturally public goods; they do not spring into being freely and openly available to all, but instead require ongoing commitment and investment in order to make and keep them that way. This commitment and investment is generous thinking made manifest. We live, however, in an era of rampant privatization, in which all manner of what were previously understood as public responsibilities have been converted to private benefit. As Michael Fabricant and Stephen Brier explore in *Austerity Blues,* public disinvestment in higher education is only one aspect of this privatization, which extends to many aspects of public, and particularly urban, infrastructure. As they note, however, the public investment that preceded this wave of privatization was not an inherent part of the democratic experiment; rather, it was produced through extraordinary struggle, "led in large part by labor unions and leftist political parties, [which] produced a shift in the roles and functions of the state. It was within this context that governmental institutions assumed more and more social responsibility for citizens" (10). That sense of social responsibility has not always been present, in other words; the period between the

Progressive Era of the late nineteenth century and the social movements of the 1960s was an unusual moment in the American development of ideas about collectivity, the social, and the public good.

That higher education in the United States most flourished during this period, however, is no accident, and it's for this reason that Newfield argues that submitting to its privatization has been academia's "great mistake." The impact of privatization on campus is evident in the degree to which core education and research functions have been outsourced to commercial enterprises. Results of this kind of outsourcing include not just McMillan Cottom's fully corporatized institutions of "lower ed," but also, in traditional institutions, key university information and processes being locked into systems that primarily serve corporate interests. This mode of privatization has resulted in the rise of what I think of as the Solutions Industry. This industry has sprung up in the gap created by universities' inability to work together to solve shared needs and the impossibility of their solving those needs individually. The Solutions Industry ostensibly provides key services that support but are not themselves central to the university's core educational mission, but it functions by rendering institutions dependent on systems that lie outside their control, and that never really work the way that would best serve institutional needs. These systems might include the course management system, the library discovery service, or even journal publishing, for that matter. Privatizing these core functions has happened over the course of decades, and for seemingly sensible reasons, but it has left the university trapped in expensive contracts that drain more than they provide institutional resources.

Beyond those particular instances of outsourcing, however, Newfield argues that "privatization has become the public university's political unconscious, in which non-economic educational means and ends lost their autonomy and become half-submerged in economic goals" (37). Privatization is in this sense not just how the cost of higher education got shifted from the government to students and parents; it is rather part and parcel of the conversion of the university's entire educational purpose to serving market-based needs: privileging research that results in patents or technology transfer; privileging educational programs that provide clearly definable career pathways. This mode of privatization is directly, demonstrably responsible for the assumption that liberal arts degrees in general, and humanities degrees most especially, are "useless."

So this chapter is filled with a number of extremely difficult questions. How might we begin to rebuild strong and flourishing ties between the university and the public good? How can we reorient institutions of higher education toward their public missions and away from the mandates of the private sector? How might we communicate the socially oriented, nonmarket value that higher education produces? And how—necessary for all of this to succeed—can we foster the understanding that our institutions will gain more from collaboration than from competition?

This is a lot to take on—especially for a poorly defined "we" who no doubt feels quite powerless before the massive bureaucracies that structure the contemporary university. Changing individual mindsets is difficult enough; changing organizational cultures and public commitments is something else altogether. It's not just a matter of a few strategic decisions and slogans here and there; it requires massive transformation, and equally massive mobilization to press for it. As Newfield convincingly argues, we cannot simply make the leap from today's heavily privatized higher education back to a fully supported public university system that provides all members of our society with the opportunity to become creative thinkers because the paradigms under which we operate today—paradigms that understand value in narrowly economistic ways and that understand the locus of that value to be the private sector—make it impossible. We cannot tear down the political unconscious that structures our institutions and their relation to the broader culture with the arguments and analytics that the current structure makes available. All those analytics lead us back to the cycle we're currently trapped in: competition, austerity, increasing privatization, and a growing divide between the university and the public it is meant to serve. Breaking that cycle and establishing a new mode of both thinking and structuring the role of the university in contemporary culture requires nothing short of a paradigm shift.

Paradigm Shift

Why a paradigm shift? Because what lies ahead requires more than simply changing a few things about the way an organization functions. Rather, it requires changing its fundamental orientation toward its goals and the ways that it strives to reach them. That reorientation is not just a matter of reiterating the values of the organization in the statements and slogans that so often cause those who work there to roll their eyes. It demands instead creating a culture within the organization that manifests those values in everything that it does. And in the case of the transformation I am attempting to describe here, it requires refusing the dominance of the privatized, economized rationality that has gotten us into the situation we currently find ourselves in. The metrics and the budgetary constraints will always push the institution away from its public orientation, away from generosity, and toward the kind of economistic comparison both among universities and with the corporate sector that our institutions can never win. But it's a comparison that we should never *want* to win. We should want to defy the profit-oriented logics of maximum efficiency, of maximum utility, of delivering value. This is not to say that we can simply refuse efficiency, utility, and value altogether, as if we live in a different world from the trustees and legislatures that ultimately control the funding of—and therefore the ability to function of—our institutions. It is, however, to say that we need to start transforming the thinking within our institutions in ways that will enable us to argue in new terms, on our own terms, for the real nonmarket, public service function of our institutions of higher education with those outside them. The very notion of the public, in fact, which most institutions have understood and oriented themselves toward only imperfectly across their histories, must be placed at the center of our thinking. When called upon to defend the value we provide to students and employers, we should do so, but in so doing, we must also always return the focus to the far more important values we model for and support in the public as a whole. This transformation in institutional thinking, this change in orientation, in vocabulary, in evidence, from a focus on value to a focus on *values*, demands a paradigm shift.

The notion of the paradigm shift derives from Thomas Kuhn's 1962 monograph, *The Structure of Scientific Revolutions*. Kuhn intended his term to illuminate something about the unfolding of the history of science—namely, that it has not proceeded through smooth, linear "progress" but instead through a series of crises and radical transformations—but the concept very quickly came to be applied to a wide range of cultural changes as well. Kuhn found himself a bit baffled by this widespread adoption, noting in a postscript to the 1969 reissue that the concept of the paradigm seemed to have "assumed a life of its own," entering common American usage in ways he didn't entirely expect (186). Perhaps as a result of this migration outside the concept's original field of reference, some of the particulars behind the notion of the paradigm shift have become a bit fuzzy. Paradigm shifts in cultural thinking do happen, certainly, but *how* they happen—and whether they can be *made* to happen—remain less clear.

Kuhn originally meant for the notion of the paradigm to serve as a synonym of sorts for the *exemplar,* the ideal example that can be used to explain or represent a more general concept or field. It came, however, to describe something closer to an ideology, a framework that structures and determines the possibilities for knowledge in general. In Kuhn's model for scientific progress, "normal science," which is largely focused on problem solving, operates under a shared paradigm, a commonly accepted model for the work underway. As Ian Hacking notes in his introduction to the fiftieth anniversary edition of *The Structure of Scientific Revolutions,* "All is well until the methods legitimated by the paradigm cannot cope with a cluster of anomalies; crisis results and persists until a new achievement redirects research and serves as a new paradigm" (xxiii). It sounds, in this description, positively orderly, but the process of establishing that new paradigm requires a revolution, a dramatic upheaval in the very basis of knowledge that displaces the old paradigm and replaces it with the new. The transition may afterward come to seem inevitable, and the textbooks may report a linear process in the development of knowledge, but the shift in thinking required of those caught in the transition is anything but simple. In the gap between the recognition of the anomalies and the emergence of the new achievement is "a period of pronounced professional insecurity" in which normal science ceases to function normally (Kuhn 68); afterward, those who have failed to make the transition to the new paradigm may be "simply read out of the profession, which thereafter ignores their work" (19). In part this happens because the old and new paradigms may mean radically different things when using the same concepts, rendering them incommensurable and leaving their adherents unable to communicate with one another.

If Christopher Newfield is correct in his assertion that a paradigm shift is necessary in order to free the university from the downward spiral that privatization has created and return it to a focus on public service, Kuhn might help us begin to understand a bit about why. The university as a whole has in recent years been laboring under two competing paradigms: an older one, largely operative within the academic community, in which the university serves as a producer and disseminator of knowledge; and a more recent one, widely subscribed to in the surrounding culture, in which the university serves as a producer and disseminator of market-oriented credentials. That is to say, while the university has proceeded over the last several decades as if it were in a period of doing, in Kuhn's sense, "normal science," a paradigm shift has already taken place all around us. This cultural transformation began during the Reagan Revolution and has only grown in force, through the Contract with America, the Tea Party, and other political movements focused on replacing the public good with private enterprise. With that political revolution has come the dramatic shift described above in popular beliefs about the education of citizens, once considered a primary obligation of society but now taken to be an individual responsibility. The paradigm that has become dominant is that of the market, within which the ideal structure is understood to be the corporation, which functions first and foremost to provide a return on investment to shareholders, and the ideal value is understood to be competition. McMillan Cottom argues that this ideological transformation has led directly to the rise of the for-profit higher education industry and the massive student debt on which it relies: "This shift away from understanding higher education as something that was important and good for society as a whole made the politics of financializing college tuition a sensible public choice" (*Lower Ed* 133). But the same thing has happened within public universities, whose strong impetus toward privatization has resulted, as Newfield explores, in a transformation that has not improved institutions' efficiency and agility as promised but instead trapped them in a downward cycle of disinvestment and debt creation. Even worse, perhaps, the intransigent belief in competition as the arbiter of the good under this market paradigm has resulted in institutions of higher education being pitted against one another rather than understanding themselves as working in solidarity for a shared social good.

Higher education's current crisis, then, stems from two key factors: on the one hand, the incommensurability of its dominant paradigm with that of the surrounding culture, and on the other, the fact that *both paradigms are failing,* if in different ways. The older paradigm holds up as its exemplar the Elite Research University, a model of influence and prestige that relies on infinite resources in order to carve out a space in which the unfettered exploration of ideas can flourish, if only for a privileged few. The newer paradigm similarly holds up high-tech, disruptive forms of enterprise education as exemplars, ranging from for-profit colleges to online instruction and credentialing, which have become models for the massive, frictionless, seemingly cost-free production of a highly skilled workforce. Neither of these paradigms can work today to create the necessary conditions for the kinds of universal education that could be provided by a university, focused on the public good, whose values exceed the economic. If those of us who work within higher education or who are genuinely concerned about its future accessibility are to create the paradigm shift necessary to make its public value visible, we first have to recognize that our paradigm has failed us. But we also need to find ways to make visible the damage that's been done by the paradigm that's taken over the culture around us.

The paradigm shift that I am arguing for thus cannot and should not be mistaken for disruption. Disruption in today's most-hyped sense is most closely associated with the work of Clayton Christensen, who coined the term "disruptive innovation" in order to describe the ways that new upstarts with new models can rapidly take over older, often inefficient, industries and markets. As an example, one might think of the effects that Uber has had on existing taxi services: looking strictly at the consumer side of the transaction, it's easy to see that in many areas it's become far more possible to get a ride, at a relatively affordable price, than ever before. On the other hand, Uber has brought with it a host of problems, including an underpaid, underregulated workforce (leading both to risks to passenger safety and to abuses of the workforce by the company) and an app that tracks user behavior in intrusive and undisclosed ways. Disruption, in other words, does not provide an alternative to the market so much as an evasion of that market's existing rules, which may set the stage for new efficiencies but may just as easily lay the groundwork for a host of new abuses. And disruption in higher education has thus far gone entirely wrong. Just as one example, the massive open online courses, or MOOCs, that were set to stand the old high-cost, in-person university on its head, delivering quality education around the world, 24/7, for little to no cost: well, they didn't. They turned out to be expensive to produce, for one thing, and to have questionable educational outcomes, especially for students who were educationally underserved in the first place. As a result, Sebastian Thrun, founder of one of the highest-profile MOOC companies, admitted as the hype began to wane that they had "a lousy product" (Chafkin). As Audrey Watters has argued time and again, such has been the story with most efforts at "ed-tech" disruption: what winds up being disrupted, more often than not, is the students (see "Myth and Millennialism" and "Ed-Tech in a Time of Trump," among many such potential sources).

What I am arguing for is thus not a disruption but a revolution in our thinking, one specifically focused on demanding the good that higher education can create: a good that is more public than private, a good that is focused primarily not on the production of economic value but instead on producing a more important range of social values. Institutions of higher education today find themselves at a most precarious crossroads; no longer content with defunding universities or slashing research support, lawmakers have begun proposing a series of increasingly intrusive measures that promise to undermine the principles under which American higher education has long operated. Measures such as these in 2017–18 included, for instance, tax reform proposals that would reclassify graduate student tuition waivers as taxable income, a move that would have rendered postgraduate education financially out of reach for all but the most wealthy. They have also included a higher education reauthorization that proposed dramatic changes to financial aid programs and increased pressure toward career outcome–based accountability. And in June 2018, the White House proposed merging the Departments of Education and Labor, making clear the functional relationship between the two in the present moment. Beyond this, lawmakers have also launched a series of interventions into personnel matters on campus, whether creating requirements for greater "ideological diversity" in hiring or demanding punitive measures against faculty members and departments perceived as taking inappropriate political positions in public. These attempts to undermine academic freedom are not driven by the desire to remove political content from campus but instead to impose the right political content: speech and instruction that promote private enterprise and the social status quo at the expense of all other social goods.

We cannot fend off this and other such attacks on the very foundations of higher education in the United States by clinging to the paradigms that have landed our institutions, and our broader culture, in this mess. In fact, the damage done by these paradigms—the damage done by our institutions' focus on prestige, and the damage done by our culture's focus on the market—manifests itself most intensely at the level of our collective self-understanding. Kuhn's model describes that ways that the failure of a scientific paradigm, as it becomes beset by anomalies for which the paradigm cannot account, throws the community that relies on that paradigm into crisis. This crisis is not just abstractly epistemological; it is a more fundamental crisis in self-understanding. A paradigm is not just a model shared by a community; it is that which makes the community a community in the first place, and as a result, "when a paradigm is threatened by crisis, the community itself is in disarray" (Hacking xxv). Recovering from this crisis requires the discovery of and commitment to a new paradigm—and that requires thoughtful experimentation and a willingness to look at the problem from a radically different angle.

Examples of experimentation in higher education exist, of course, but many of their outcomes are as yet questionable, as they continue to work within the existing paradigm. Michael Crow, for instance, has worked very consciously at Arizona State University to produce a new exemplar for what he deems the New American University, and in so doing he has enabled the university to vastly expand access and to create innovative ways of thinking about institutional and curricular structure. And yet this model, with its heavy focus on public-private partnerships, is a bit limited in the ways that it can transform public thinking about, and public investment in, the university. It's a model in which the public good seems equated with service to the new economy. And it's a model in which market-based competition reigns. This new paradigm makes some of the strengths of the Elite Research University available to many more students with far more socioeconomically diverse backgrounds, thus undermining the sense in which "prestige is attained through the maintenance of scarcity" (Crow and Dabars 30). However, in its heavy focus on entrepreneurialism and in its relentless assessment of excellence through national standings, growth in research funding, numbers of Nobel laureates, and the like, the New American University winds up merging aspects of the Elite Research University's prestige with market-focused quality indicators, leaving the institution entirely dependent upon a paradigm that drives inexorably toward privatization.

If we are in fact ready to recognize that the university is in a profound crisis of the type that Kuhn describes—one in which "normal science" is decreasingly possible, in which the community itself is in disarray—we should not look for solutions within our existing models, but rather begin developing new models for understanding how what we do works. That is, we need alternatives both to the Elite Research University paradigm and to the market-driven quality paradigm. Rather than reconceiving the university itself as a new form of semi-public, semi-corporate enterprise capable of producing a more egalitarian Harvard, we need to begin from an entirely different standpoint. Our dominant narratives about the rise to preeminence of the American system of higher education place that system's birth in 1876, with the merger of the Oxbridge-style undergraduate college and the German-derived graduate/research institution in the founding of Johns Hopkins University. An entirely different view of that system might become possible if we were instead to begin our narrative with a different birthplace: the 1862 Morrill Act, which established the land-grant system of state agricultural and mechanical colleges, charged with promoting "the liberal and practical education of the industrial classes in the several pursuits and professions in life" (7 U.S. Code § 304). The land-grant model has been far from perfect—it's important not to forget that the land so "granted" was first seized from the indigenous people who had long inhabited it, and however egalitarian these institutions may have tried to become, the founding ideas of the citizenry they were intended to serve were far from inclusive. But the public focus of these institutions has in many cases pressed them, over their histories, to do better. A new focus for today's universities, and a new will to continue doing better, might emerge if we understand the founding mission of higher education in the United States not to have been educating those destined for conventional forms of leadership, but rather educating those who might help their communities grow from the grassroots up.

There are, of course, a host of other voluntary communities and educational cooperatives that have similarly addressed the needs that arise from people's actual lives rather than from the desire to oversee and manage those lives at scale. These alternative models include the public "Conversations" held by Margaret Fuller in early nineteenth-century Boston, which were designed to support women in learning despite their exclusion from conventional institutions of higher education (Zwarg). They also include the lyceum movement, which brought educational programming to communities across the country in the years leading up to the Civil War, as well as the twentieth-century labor colleges and folk schools that supported union organizers, civil rights workers, and others working toward social justice within their communities (Bradbury; Horton and Freire). Models such as these might lead us to suspect that what we need may be less an innovation in the delivery system for higher education today than a new conception of the community that we are building both within our institutions and between those institutions and the public they should serve.

Community

Thinking about our own understanding of community—both the community that the university *is* and the community within which the university operates—might return us briefly to Kuhn and his interest in the ways that scientific revolutions operate in part by throwing the scientific community into crisis. Kuhn suggests that paradigm shifts very often require transformations in the community itself, precisely because of its members' attachment to the ways that things have been done. It's thus no accident that paradigm shifts frequently align with generational change, as the new discoveries required to create new paradigms are commonly uncovered by "men so young or so new to the crisis-ridden field that practice has committed them less deeply than most of their contemporaries to the world view and rules determined by the old paradigm" (Kuhn 143). Undoubtedly so. And yet, in reading *The Structure of Scientific Revolutions* today, it's impossible to avoid the degree to which the community remains precisely the same throughout: not "men" as a now-antiquated ostensibly neutral term for "people," but *men*. Not a single woman is mentioned throughout the volume. It took later feminist and other critical approaches to the history and sociology of science to begin to make the effects of this gap clear. As Sandra Harding argues in *Whose Science? Whose Knowledge?*, in addition to telling us empirically verifiable things about the world, science has always also been "politics by other means," and the failure to be conscious of those politics has led to limitations in what science can do (10). In fact, Harding notes, the conception of the natural sciences as the epitome of objectivity and rationality has hampered the development of sciences "that are not systematically blinded to the ways in which their descriptions and explanations of their subject matters are shaped by the origins and consequences of their research practices and by the interests, desires, and values promoted by such practices" (15). Science—like all forms of academic research—may aspire to objectivity, but it has always been conducted by humans, who are inescapably subjective beings. What has been required in order to create the kind of paradigm shift that allows us to see that subjectivity and its effects—the kind of paradigm shift that can genuinely affect not just the results but the very practice of academic work—is, as this chapter's epigraph from Tressie McMillan Cottom suggests, not a new tool or a new technique or a new method, but a new politics.

This is as broadly true of the institutions of higher education that host the work as it is of the work undertaken within particular academic fields. As Mary Beard notes in *Women and Power*,

"You cannot easily fit women into a structure that is already coded as male; you have to change the structure. That means thinking about power differently. It means decoupling it from prestige. It means thinking collaboratively, about the power of followers not just of leaders" (86–87). And so of difference of many kinds: you cannot easily fit people of color into a structure that is already coded as white, not if you are trying to create an institution that genuinely reflects the needs and interests of the entirety of the community. Instead, you must change the structure and its coding in ways that make not just diversity but genuine inclusivity possible. This type of change requires a willingness to think about the institution's often unspoken structural biases; it is not just a matter of making it possible for more kinds of people to achieve conventionally coded success within the institution, but instead of examining what constitutes success, how it is measured, and why. It requires thinking first and foremost about values, as well as about the ways those values are instantiated in the processes through which the institution operates.

Among those values that need examination, as I hope the preceding discussion suggests, is prestige: how it is defined, how it is awarded, how it is withheld. As the provost whose talk opened this chapter laid bare, prestige is a competitive matter, with a singular goal, and the quest for it is one of the things that isolates our institutions both from one another and from their communities. In seeking prestige, we reinforce hierarchy and exclusion. And so, *pace* Beard, in decoupling power from prestige, we need not just to think about followers, but also to reconsider what it is we focus on when we talk about leaders, and why we think of the nonelite as "followers" in the first place. What if, instead of leaders and followers, we were able to focus our attention on the building and sustenance of communities, of collectives working together toward common goals? How might such a shift in focus transform the educational mission, as well as the structural objectives, of institutions of higher education? Conventionally, thinking about universities' role in the development of "tomorrow's leaders" means focusing on (or hoping for) the production of future CEOs and elected officials, individuals with the kinds of power and prestige that might reflect on (and, in those hopes, be brought to the future assistance of) the institutions from which they came. If universities were instead to focus on the development of communities, the mode of leadership they educate for might be grounded less in prestige—in individualistic markers of power—than in connection and collaboration.

This need for a focus on community has given rise to several of the alternative models for higher education I mentioned a moment ago. Myles Horton, for instance, in thinking about the purposes and goals of the Highlander Folk Institute, noted the purposeful decision he'd made not to work within traditional institutions of higher education, but instead to seek ways of "working with emerging community leaders or organizational leaders, to try to help those people get a vision and some understanding of how you go about realizing that vision so that they could go back into their communities and spread the ideas" (Horton and Freire 184). In order to make this possible, Highlander had to dismantle conventional understandings of education and allow the work to be driven by the needs and concerns of the people involved. But translating this cooperative mode of engagement to more traditional institutions of higher education requires not just new pedagogies, or new internal structures; it requires a new paradigm, even a new political unconscious: a turn from privatized, rationalist, competition-based models for knowledge production to ways of knowing, of learning, of being in community that are grounded in an ethic of care.

Feminist care ethics derives primarily from the work of Carol Gilligan and Nel Noddings, who proposed caring as an alternative to rationalist ethical models focused on objective principles. As Noddings describes them, these models, typified by Lawrence Kohlberg's stages of moral development, argue that individual moral reasoning progresses from self-interest, through interpersonal relations, to abstract ethical principles; such models suggest that women are less highly developed as moral beings because their judgment is based less on universal ideas and more on intimate human connections and feelings. Gilligan and Noddings argue, by contrast, that focusing on women's grounding in interpersonal relationships and resulting personal responsibilities might enable the development of "a powerful and coherent ethic and, indeed, a different sort of world" from the male-dominated rational-objective world of principles (Noddings 92). This ethic is one based not in universalized notions of right and wrong but rather in the obligations that each of us bear to care for those around us who are in need. Key to that ethic is receptivity: both the openness of what Noddings refers to as the "one-caring" to the needs of the other, and the openness of the "cared-for" to the care being provided. This position of receptivity bears a great deal in common with the listening practices that I emphasized in chapter 1, including a willingness to attend to the other, to hear their concerns, and to act as best as possible in consideration of the needs expressed. In that discussion of listening, however, I focused on the obligation that each of us bears individually to those around us. What I would now like us to consider is how the university might become a more receptive institution, more attuned to the needs of the communities that should form its cared-for. How might the university, both internally and externally, become a caring community?

There are some risks associated with focusing an institution or a community around principles of care, perhaps needless to say. The need around us is infinite, and as Noddings notes, the thought of meeting such need is sufficiently overwhelming that as individuals we are faced with "the temptation to withdraw from the public domain" and to focus on our own internal requirements. This is perhaps part of the reason the university finds itself in its current predicament: unable to meet all the need by which it is surrounded and under relentless examination by a rationalist culture, the institution turns inward, becoming hermetic and isolated, and the individuals who nonetheless try to fill those needs from within the institution face burnout. However, while the ethic of care creates an obligation to connect, that obligation is not unbounded: "We cannot care for everyone. Caring itself is reduced to mere talk about caring when we attempt to do so" (Noddings 145). The obligation is greatest when it is closest to home. In fact, the further from home we attempt to extend our concern, the more likely that caring-for will devolve into what Noddings calls "caring about," a more abstracted position in which any obligation can be readily dismissed: "'Caring about' always involves a certain benign neglect. One is attentive just so far. One assents with just so much enthusiasm. One acknowledges. One affirms. One contributes five dollars and goes on to other things" (181). Caring-about seems to be the primary mode in which the university usually operates with respect to its surrounding community: making a largely symbolic contribution, feeling good about it, and moving on. True caring requires remaining in relation, genuinely becoming part of a community, while recognizing and acknowledging the limitations involved in doing so. I'll discuss some examples shortly of ways that the university might become a more receptive institution, more attuned to and guided by the needs around it.

But I'll also need to talk about ways that the university, in becoming more receptive to the community around it, must also develop an internal receptivity, an internal sense of community as well. Because the risks associated with creating a caring community do not lie solely in the institution's inability to meet an infinite external need, but also in the unequal distribution of caring responsibilities. It hardly needs to be pointed out that Western culture places far greater demands for caring on women rather than men. And while Noddings and Gilligan derive their arguments about care from feminist ideals of connection and relation, other critics, including Nancy Chodorow, have argued that the reproduction of the caring relationship typified by mothering works to reinforce rather than subvert patriarchal social structures. Faculty members have long seen that danger in operation within the university, as women and faculty of color take on a disproportionate share of the care-related activity involved in mentoring and other forms of service within the institution. This work is often profoundly meaningful to the individuals involved, and yet the time and energy devoted to care risks causing individual scholars to lose competitiveness within their cohorts every bit as much as the provost at the chapter's outset projected it would for an institution writ large. As long as faculty success is organized around individual competition—as long as universities' incentives and reward structures are largely focused on valorizing individual labor toward competitive ends—community-oriented activities will fall to those of lower status, and will perpetuate that hierarchy. The response to this form of inequity has often been the strong advice to women and faculty of color to say no, to refuse the labor of caring, to protect their time, to demand equal access to the individualistic, competitive focus that the institution rewards. Noddings notes that this response is in many ways the path of least resistance: "In an age concerned with equity and justice—and far less concerned with relatedness and cooperation—we shall almost surely find it easier to join men in their traditional ways than to induce them to join us" (190). But it is also a path that leads away from community, that prevents connection, that leaves the university and its members caught up in the mandate to compete all the time. Instead, as Mary Beard suggests, we have to change the structure. In turning the institution toward outwardly expressed forms of care for its community, we must also turn it toward inwardly expressed forms of care, including ensuring that demands for emotional and relational labor within the university are equitably distributed and, most importantly, ensuring that such labor is prioritized and rewarded. And this, as I'll discuss in a bit, requires standing the institution's assessment practices on their heads: creating a caring community by becoming a community that genuinely values care.

In order to become such a community, as Dara Regaignon reminded me in the discussion of the draft of this book, the university would need to be willing to slow down, to take time to connect, to allow for conversation, to linger in dissensus. Time is an increasingly scarce resource for all of us, however; there is no time available to us to reflect, to listen, not when our next annual review is coming due, in which we have to demonstrate outputs rather than understanding. Maggie Berg and Barbara Seeber argue in their book, *The Slow Professor,* that rescuing the university from the corporatized strictures and processes in which it has become mired requires not an escape from everyday life but rather a willingness to live the everyday with care and attention—but that care and attention require us all to be willing to slow down, to step out of the temporality that has been conditioned by the mandate to compete all the time. That speed, as the proverb suggests, requires each of us to go alone; if we are willing to slow down, however, and go together instead—to collaborate, to work as a community—we have the potential to go far.

This is true not only within institutional communities but between them as well. There are important potential benefits that might derive from colleges and universities together understanding themselves to be a community rather than existing primarily in competition with one another. Individual institutions cannot themselves solve the problems faced in today's libraries, for instance—such as the need to balance preservation of print collections with demands on the space they require, or the need to provide digital access to collections while contending with the labor and infrastructure requirements involved in doing so—but working together, solutions (rather than Solutions) might be found. Some not-for-profit organizations such as HathiTrust and some informal collectives such as the Future of the Print Record working group are trying to point the way, but ensuring that the not-for-profits are adequately supported to be able to take on such a monumental task and that the collectives become more formalized collaborations remains a challenge ("Concerted Thought"). And the challenge remains, not least, because the library is one of the key areas of competition among universities, a point of invidious comparison that keeps institutions fighting for prestige rather than building community.

It is in focusing on community at all levels, rather than on particular skills or fields of knowledge, that I believe the university can make its greatest contribution to its culture, helping to ensure that we become a strong, functioning democracy. Scholars such as Martha Nussbaum have pointed to the role of the humanities—especially philosophy, history, and literature—in cultivating "the ability to think critically; the ability to transcend local loyalties and to approach world problems as a 'citizen of the world'; and, finally, the ability to imagine sympathetically the predicament of another person," abilities that are, she argues, "crucial to the health of any democracy internally, and to the creation of a decent world culture capable of constructively addressing the world's most pressing problems" (7). And these fields do have key roles to play in creating thoughtful, well-rounded citizens capable of responding with care to difficult and, today, often dangerous issues that we face together. But those abilities alone cannot be enough; the study of philosophy, history, and literature (or music, or art, or theater) may expose students to the possibility of empathetic connection but such studies cannot in and of themselves instill the value of connection in ways that can genuinely transform a community or a culture. Part of the problem in making that transfer may stem from our mistaken understanding of what it is to build a strong, functioning democracy. As I mentioned earlier, the university's focus has long been on preparing "tomorrow's leaders," and so we often conflate preparation for democracy with preparation for leadership, for decision-making. But the key element of a working democracy may not be strong leaders at the top, but a strong *demos*—ordinary citizens—who can organize at the grassroots level around their own concerns, and who are willing both to ensure that their concerns are heard and to care for the often quite different concerns of others. What this suggests is that the university should focus less energy on educating for leadership and more on educating for community.

Possibilities

This sense of education for community is inseparable from the public-service mission of most state-supported, land-grant universities in the United States, but perhaps the best-articulated version of that mission and its possibilities lies in the Wisconsin Idea. This complex of initiatives was an experiment in democracy in which "the extensive use of academic and other experts in government, agriculture, and industry, and an enlightened electorate were all prominent elements" (Carstensen 181). The origins of the Wisconsin Idea lie, in fact, in one of the weaknesses of the land-grant proposal; in Wisconsin, as in several other states, attempts to draw farmers into the agricultural education programs provided by the university had largely failed, in part because those programs were seen as too theoretical and too removed from the practical. In order to fend off an attempt by farm groups to create their own agricultural school, the university began in the late nineteenth century to offer a series of short courses, held throughout the state, that "gave the professors the chance to talk to the farmers and, what was perhaps more important, gave the farmers a chance to talk back" (183). The success of these short courses led to others oriented toward mechanics and industry, and finally to the radical notion that "what could be done in the field of practical education could be done in the field of liberal education" (184). These courses experienced varying levels of uptake, but they provided the first glimpses of what an extension program designed to bring university education out into the state might accomplish. The result, at the turn of the twentieth century, under Governor Robert LaFollette and university president Charles Van Hise, was a set of political and educational reforms that brought experts from the university into direct public service, advising on a range of issues faced within the state. These reforms also established the university's extension division, which focused on providing the people of the state with the education they needed, where and when they needed it, in the form best suited to their purposes. This division was not adjunct to but a central element of the university as a state institution. As Van Hise noted in a 1905 address, the university is and should be focused on the needs of the people, both through its extension into the community and through its on-campus programs. A university, he argued, does not exist for the benefit of those who work there, and "it is not even mainly supported for the direct benefit of the students who take advantage of its opportunities. It is supported that they may become better fitted to serve the state and the nation" (5). *Serve,* not lead. The purpose of the university, as coalesced within the Wisconsin Idea, was first and foremost research and education in service to the entire population of the state.

Of course, these innovations were made possible by a very different political moment from ours, a progressive era in which reformers sought "to make government more responsive to the will of the people," rather than the other way around (Carstensen 187). And one of their key problems, as Steve Brier pointed out in our online discussion of the draft of this book, is that Progressive Era reforms such as these were dependent on the reformers at the top. Rather than building a fully empowered community that would sustain the institution, the continued focus on educating individuals under the Wisconsin Idea left an opening for LaFollette and Van Hise's vision to be undone by a later generation of leaders. But the principles behind the Wisconsin Idea remain, particularly as they establish a focus for university priorities, and they might be drawn upon as a means of thinking about how the contemporary relevance of the university might be reestablished, how the university might be integrated into the life of its community, and how the sense of its community might be extended throughout the state, and even the nation. This requires more than just a new public-relations campaign. Rather, building real connections to and within the community must be part of a long-term project of rededicating the institution to its public mission, in ways that both focus its efforts and invite public involvement and even ownership of its programs. Today, it seems, the primary point of identification with the state university for most residents is its major sports teams. By and large, the faculty hate this, of course, and recent studies have shown that the vast majority of athletics programs draw resources away from other areas of the university, rather than being the revenue pipeline so often imagined (Hobson and Rich; Wolverton et al.). But the research and instructional units within the university have provided few alternative means of fostering and maintaining such identification within the community, and it's there that the university's efforts must focus.

What kinds of programs might provide these opportunities for identification today? What might a university extension program for the twenty-first century look like? At the University of Wisconsin–Madison, programs such as these remain part of the institution's infrastructure. The UniverCity Alliance, for instance, supports local governments throughout the state as they seek to make their communities more sustainable, inclusive, healthy, and livable, by bringing together teams of faculty and students to consult on and assist with locally determined priorities ("UniverCity Alliance"). The alliance grows out of the recognition that while the desire for change within local communities is often strong, the capacity for that change—whether measured in new ideas or staff time—is often constrained. As the program notes, however, students have an abundance of creativity and desire to make change, and so bringing them into collaboration with city officials, with the oversight of faculty researchers in a range of fields from across the university, can provide the ground for fruitful conversation and action. Moreover, it provides students with hands-on experience in public service as a core component of their education. The UniverCity Alliance thus provides a framework matching city needs and desires with university expertise and energy, ensuring that both municipal priorities for change and university educational objectives are met.

A project such as the UniverCity Alliance is a relatively easy reach for the academic fields that are involved in the collaboration, including urban planning, landscape architecture, economics, public administration, and the like, all of which focus explicitly on various aspects of place-based policy and practice. There are, however, programs bringing other, less obvious forms of university expertise to bear in communities as well. The University of Wisconsin's Center for the Humanities has for the last twelve years, for instance, hosted its Great World Texts program, bringing students and teachers across the state together in reading and discussing a "classic piece of literature," through colloquia for teachers, student conferences, and the creation of a shared set of instructional resources ("Great World Texts"). Similarly, the Music Engagement and Outreach program of the School of Music not only sends three of the school's ensembles to perform in schools and concert halls throughout the state but also provides instruction, mentoring, and collaboration between music faculty and student musicians ("Engagement and Outreach"). All of these programs, and the many more like them, are meant to embody the Wisconsin Idea in action: the notion that the university's expertise has been gathered not to improve the institution's own status but to support the education and well-being of the people in the state and across the nation.

It's impossible to let this discussion of the Wisconsin Idea pass, however, without a bit of attention to what's happened to it in recent years. Most famously, Republican Governor Scott Walker in 2015 launched what one columnist referred to as "a two-pronged attack" on the university, slashing its budget and proposing to eliminate tenure (Salzburg). These maneuvers were interpreted by faculty and students alike as an attack on academic freedom, and in particular as an attempt to silence what is popularly understood as a bastion of liberalism within public life. One particularly damaging result for the university was an exodus of faculty, as they were "poached" by other institutions—competitors, straight out of the privatization paradigm—that could provide less risky, and more supported, working conditions. Similar interventions into the workings of state universities have been made by politicians across the nation, whether directly or through politically appointed trustees, who have at one and the same time radically decreased state financial support to higher education and significantly stepped up their intrusions into university governance. To see this happen in Wisconsin, however, after a century characterized by strong bonds between the university and the state under the Wisconsin Idea, has been profoundly dismaying. We live in an age, it seemed to say, in which no amount of generous care for community on the part of the university can overcome the political ambitions of elected officials determined to fully implement their visions of a nation dominated by private enterprise and, in order to do so, eliminate their opposition. What *can* overcome those ambitions, however, is an infuriated and organized electorate. As the editor of a central Wisconsin newspaper noted, "People take a lot of pride in U.W.-Madison—it's one of the

crown jewels of the state" (Bosman). The full impact of continuing budget reductions and required restructuring is still making
itself felt, but that felt attachment to the university, and the sense
in which the people of the state have benefitted from its programs,
is one of the institution's greatest assets, and should not be
underestimated.

My own institution, Michigan State University, faces all of the
same challenges to its public service mission as do its land-grant
peers across the nation. But it also faces today an entirely different kind of crisis, the results of a betrayal of the public trust
through a massive abdication of the duty of care. And it is important not to diminish the extent to which such care is a duty owed
by the institution both to its internal community—especially its
students—and to the world. MSU, founded in 1855 as the Agricultural College of the State of Michigan, was the prototype for
the land-grant institutions established by the Morrill Act of 1862,
and the university calls daily upon the public-service mission implied by that role for orientation and focus. My original plan, at
this point in the chapter, was to turn to talking about some of the
recent programs developed here on campus that have built on the
institution's public-service legacy. But it's impossible to talk about
MSU in 2018 without talking about its other legacy, the Larry Nas-
sar case, in which a member of the medical faculty and gymnastics team doctor (who was also, horrifically, the team doctor for
the US Olympic gymnastics team) was revealed to have sexually
abused literally hundreds of young women over the course of decades, including many *after* the first accusations had been made.
The university is, as I write, under more investigations than I can
count, by both federal and state authorities, and faces potential
criminal charges in addition to enormous civil liability. The university president has resigned in disgrace, and the faculty senate

has passed a vote of no confidence in the entirety of the board of trustees. Much of the external investigation is aimed at uncovering who knew what when, attempting to determine the precise level of blame and the appropriate targets for it. I would argue, however, that the blame is and ought to be limitless—even if members of the upper administration did not know, they remain responsible, and especially for the not-knowing. And I would also argue that while individuals must be held accountable for their actions and inactions, the target of blame must be the institution itself. The abdication of the duty of care is systemic, not (or not solely) personal. It is a massive failure encoded into the very structures and policies of the university, structures and policies whose goal, as in many institutions across the country, is to protect the institution rather than the individuals within it, and this has resulted in an incalculable human cost.

The people who make up the MSU community—the faculty and staff and students and alumni—continue to work as hard as they can to do good for the institution and for the world. There are programs that seek to cultivate new kinds of connections, through both research and teaching, between the university and the public. Citizen Scholars, for instance, a program launched in the fall of 2016, is designed not just to get students out into experiential or service learning opportunities in Michigan but rather to connect their on-campus learning with the community in ways that can help build citizen leadership from the grassroots up. Citizen Scholars is focused on "fostering the next generation of civically engaged, socially conscious, creative and innovative thinkers" by cultivating critical thinking, ethical imagination, and cultural awareness ("Citizen Scholars"). Students, who may enroll in any major within the College of Arts & Letters, are provided with both financial and personal support as they determine and work toward their academic and civic goals, including support for internships and study abroad/away experiences. More than anything, students are encouraged to understand their educational processes as focused not just on self-enrichment but also on the communal good that they can build. The program actively encourages collaboration and peer mentoring, working to create a community among the students at the same time that it connects those students with the world. That sense of community building points toward one of the program's key aspects: students are encouraged to develop high aspirations for connecting their academic and civic lives, and they are rewarded with financial support and enrichment opportunities for having done so—but those rewards in turn create higher expectations for the students, who are challenged to bring the knowledge and experience they have developed back to the program and to remain connected through the program's alumni network.

And like the University of Wisconsin and most other land-grant institutions, MSU has an extension program that brings university resources to communities across the state. The extension program is primarily focused on agriculture, natural resources, and health care, and thus primarily serves the state's farm communities and other rural areas. However, the university has also created a broad series of partnerships within the city of Detroit, focusing on challenges ranging from urban agriculture and reforestation to improving student college readiness, along with a range of arts and education-oriented programs ("Detroit Stories"). These programs include DETxMSU, which in the summer of 2016 brought sixty students from across MSU to Detroit to learn from and partner with groups throughout the city and contribute to a wide variety of projects. The key to these partnerships was, as in the UniverCity Alliance, finding out what the groups in Detroit actually want to do. Joshua Sapotichne, a member of the MSU political science faculty and coordinator of one of the DETxMSU programs, noted that many such programs founder because of the extent to which they "paratroop" students in for brief periods of time to help with problems they don't fully understand. He went on to note that rather than saying "'We're from MSU and here to help,' we asked, 'What do you need? How we can help?' These are the kind of conversations we had for months prior to when we started . . . so the work the students are doing has a lasting impact" (Kozlowski). Among the organizations that students worked with in the course of the program was the Detroit Historical Society; Nathan Kelber, who was manager of digital projects for the society during summer 2016, shared via email that the two students who worked with his team helped to digitize and transcribe materials that enabled the society to tell key parts of the story of Detroit's history and preserve it for future generations.

These efforts to build community-based partnerships are of course not restricted to MSU students; many faculty members are engaged in developing programs such as these or in research that directly involves surrounding communities. Dawn Opel, for instance, a faculty member in Writing, Rhetoric, and American Culture, is leading a study designed to help clinicians at the medical center work with partners in the community such as social services organizations in order to better coordinate and communicate health care plans ("Improving Health Care"). Bringing insights from rhetoric and user experience design to bear on contemporary health care communication has the potential to greatly improve the ways that providers and patients connect around matters of enormous importance. Similarly, Gordon Henry, a professor in English and an enrolled member of the White Earth Anishinaabe Nation in Minnesota, is the founder of Indigistory, a collaborative partnership between the Inter-Tribal Council of Michigan, the Saginaw Chippewa Tribal College, the Michigan History Center, and several units at MSU, including the College of Arts & Letters, the Native American Institute, and the MSU Hub for Innovation in Learning and Technology. Indigistory provides Native American community members, especially young adults, with support and resources to produce short digital films about their families and communities ("Indigistory"). And—just one more from among many possible examples—Christopher Long, dean of the College of Arts & Letters, has led the development of the *Public Philosophy Journal,* an open publication employing a process of "formative peer review" designed to create partnerships between academic and public thinkers working on questions of deep public concern, with the goal of creating scholarship that is "accessible to, relevant for, and shaped by the public" ("About"). These forms of collaboration, focused on community needs, community voices, and community participation, have the potential to help reshape the ways that the broader public understands the university.

Institution

But even so: MSU cannot help but demonstrate the extent to which a university can invest in any number of positive community-oriented educational and research programs and still be riddled with massive internal ignorance of or, worse, knowing indifference to the ways that its systems and structures fail to uphold the values that the institution professes. No amount of service learning or community-engaged research has thus far succeeded in transforming the structure of our institutions—any of our institutions—or the ways they are perceived and experienced by the public in general. If anything, we lay the groundwork for an inevitable betrayal of the public trust every time we focus on building such programs without building corresponding internal policies and structures in line with them. To some extent, this is about resources, of course: sustaining a program such as DETxMSU over the long term remains a challenge because it's the kind of program that is easy to celebrate as a nice grant-funded co-curricular addition to the university rather than understanding it to lie at the heart of the university's mission. But it's also about what we value in a less material sense. If the prime directive is to protect the institution at all costs, people who question institutional practices or who bring to light institutional failures will be silenced. But if the prime directive is instead to build and protect the community and all of its members, both inside and outside the institution, we need new institutional policies and practices that manifest that value.

As my conversation with that provost that I described at the beginning of this chapter makes clear, a university's assessment practices are one of the places where the actual values of an institution are most emphatically expressed. If we encourage faculty members to develop open, innovative, community-focused projects, for instance, but then continue to privilege conventional forms of scholarly production such as the book and the journal article when it comes to merit and promotion reviews, we wind up reinforcing the view that inward-facing communication and traditional markers of excellence are all that really matter. Changing that value structure requires not just developing outward-facing university initiatives but attuning the institution's assessment practices toward them. We must find ways, that is, of placing our value where our values are. But this is more than just a matter of rewriting a few policies and restructuring a few forms; it requires a thorough institutional self-examination and a real rethinking of the nature of assessment itself. As Nel Noddings notes, "Our approaches to creativity and caring"—approaches that render them marginal within lives defined by production and competition—"are induced by the dominating insistency on objective evaluation. How can we emphasize the receptivity that is at the core of both when we have no way of measuring it?" (60). This crucial problem arises in no small part from the nature of measurement and the ways we understand it: our tools for measurement privilege the measurable. Where we attempt to develop instruments for assessment that remove seemingly dangerous forms of human subjectivity and judgment in a laudable effort to make our processes objective, we inevitably wind up counting things. There's nothing necessarily wrong with counting things; some things demand to be counted. The problem is that we wind up choosing things to count precisely because they *can be counted*, not because they *matter*. And as long as our assessment practices remain caught within a paradigm that privileges competition and prestige above all else, so will our institutions.

But what alternative do we have? How can we ensure that we're counting the things that ought to count, and even more, how can we ground our assessment practices in things that matter, even when they can't be counted? And how do we get past the difficulty of motivating a group of people who have succeeded under one set of standards and incentive structures to contemplate changing those standards and structures without automatically assuming that *changing* standards means *lowering* them? This is a challenge being explored by team behind the Humane Metrics in the Humanities and Social Sciences (HuMetricsHSS) initiative, a group of researchers in the United States and Europe conducting their

research under a grant awarded to MSU by the Andrew W. Mel-
lon Foundation. The initiative describes its goals as "rethinking
humane indicators of excellence in the humanities and social
sciences" by focusing on "a values-based framework for understanding and evaluating all aspects of the scholarly life well-lived
and for promoting the nurturing of these values in scholarly
practice" ("About HuMetricsHSS"). The team's process includes
conducting a series of workshops that ask participants to articulate and discuss their most deeply held values and then imagine
how those values might be manifested in scholarly practices such
as publications, syllabi, and other outputs. The team began the
research project with five articulated values—collegiality, quality,
equity, openness, and community—but they acknowledged a
key problem in the project's design: "Could we presume these
values were universal, and might we craft a framework that allowed for adaptability if not universality?" (Jason Rhody). That
framework is still in development, and of course how it might be
taken up within institutions remains to be seen. However, one of
the principal investigators on this grant is Christopher Long, dean
of the College of Arts & Letters at MSU, who began the project
hoping to make the college a test bed for the implementation
of such a values-oriented assessment framework as it becomes
available.

This project presents one possibility for real, thoroughgoing
institutional change. I'd argue, in fact, that the present crisis at
MSU might suggest that our own assessment practices are a necessary place to begin, because educating for community requires
prior attention to our own community, refocusing the university
on its very existence as a community with a public mission. The
work of refocusing the university—of creating the paradigm shift
that can direct our efforts toward new goals and new models for

who and what we aspire to become—will at some point require administrative buy-in, of course, but it must begin with the faculty, working individually and collectively through their programs, departments, and colleges to demand a transformation in the structure and purposes of assessment, to insist upon the rejection of hierarchies based on competition and prestige. As Fabricant and Brier argue, the faculty must "evolve into something more than frustrated bystanders in the remaking of the public university" (293). When I say that this transformation must begin with the faculty, however, I do not mean to imply that the faculty can or should accomplish anything without the staff, the students, and the other committed members of the university community. Rather, faculty members, more than any other segment of the university community, tend to understand themselves as free agents, independent operators not beholden to—and all too frequently alienated from—the institution as a whole. We as faculty must begin precisely by recommitting ourselves to the institutional community and its future, and by building solidarity with staff and students, in order to ensure that all of us will have a future to share.

That the faculty have this ability to begin such a process of institutional transformation, in an era of increasingly attenuated faculty governance, is of course not a given, but they should. As William G. Bowen and Eugene M. Tobin remind us in their study of faculty governance in higher education, the American Association of University Professors in 1915 "asserted clearly that faculty 'are the appointees, but not in any proper sense the employees,' of universities; the example of judges was cited. The argument was that these appointees were responsible to a wider public, not just to their own trustees, for the fulfillment of the social function of the university" (43). The faculty, in fact, is the beneficiary of and has been entrusted with the nonmarket social benefits that higher education can provide; as such, our primary loyalty must be to those for whom we hold those benefits in trust. We have to take responsibility for transforming our institutions—and for demonstrating as broadly and as publicly as possible the common good that those institutions serve—in order to ensure that such a common good continues to exist.

The question arises, of course: What happens if we don't reorient our institutions to make them more communally and collectively focused, more worthy of the public trust? Maybe nothing. Maybe we'll get lucky, and in the next election cycle a wave of outrage from the marginalized and disenfranchised will sweep in new progressive-minded legislators and other elected officials, who understand the deep communal purposes that the university, properly supported, can serve. But maybe we won't get that lucky. Maybe the current cycle of privatization and corporatization in higher education will simply continue, or even accelerate, and more new institutions that claim to serve the private goods of career preparation and individual enrichment will arise, profiting from public needs and anxieties. Some such institutions will fail, some will succeed, but all will undermine the purposes and preeminence of public-oriented American higher education as we have known it.

If that often-idealized form of higher education is to survive, if it is to continue serving needs beyond those of the market, it must be rooted in community, and in care for that community. Care, as Noddings notes, is not just about feeling but about "relating and remaining related" (84). It is about creating and sustaining structures of communal and collective life that can endure. Such care is not just an obligation of individuals but of institutions: universities writ large must begin to think about their own relationships with one another as well, about the extent to which, rather than being in competition, they must understand themselves as interdependent. All of us—faculty, staff, students, parents, and the institutions that we rely upon—have more to gain from working together, from understanding ourselves and our institutions as intimately connected, than we have to lose in market share.

The Path Forward

Instead of thinking of publics as static or passive
entities, we could think of them as forms of energy,
made up of a multiplicity of diverse and finite people
seeking together to find a path forward.
—**NOËLLE MCAFEE,** "PUBLIC KNOWLEDGE"

On November 3, 2004, I found myself standing in front of
my Introduction to Media Studies class, not at all sure what
to say. My students were mostly first- and second-year students,
and the presidential election that had been held the day before
was the first moment of real political activity in which many of
them had been engaged. They'd canvassed and phone banked and
otherwise gotten involved, and many of them were crushed—if
not in tears, giving every impression of having been quite recently, or of being on the verge. And so I stood there and tried to
figure out what I could say that might make any difference to
them at all.

I told them about my first semester of college and the morn-
ing in November 1984 when my American Government professor walked in, said "I don't want to talk about it," and went on with
his regularly scheduled lecture. And I told them that I finally understood something about how he felt.

But I also told them that early information emerging from the
exit polls conducted the day before suggested that the division
visible in the country's voting patterns correlated strongly with

disparities both in educational level and in sources of media consumption, thus pointing to the screaming need in the United States for more, better education, especially around media literacy. And so, I told them, while the result of the election did not give me hope—far from it—it did give me purpose, a purpose that was not just about me sharing knowledge with them, but about encouraging them to develop the commitment necessary to pass that knowledge on as well.

And we went back to work.

I have tried, more or less every day since November 9, 2016, to remember that moment, that certainty that even in the midst of despair there was work to be done, and that it was my job to do some small part of it. That doing the work was the way forward. But it has been hard: hard to show up in the face of mounting horrors, hard to feel like the work that is in my sphere can have any effect on it at all. Hard, in fact, not to feel like the work I'd committed myself to in 2004 had failed, abysmally. I am not a community organizer; far from it. I am an academic, and a pretty introverted one at that. But if my job is not single-handedly creating the caring community I long for, but rather finding ways to help others—to help *you*—join in the process of creating it, it's possible that there is still something I can do. I can show up, and I can help make it possible for you show up, too.

It's hard to know how to take action in the midst of such impossible opposition, in the face of such immovable institutions, surrounded by such a sense of cultural disintegration. It's hard to imagine paths forward at a moment of such profound despair. But as Ta-Nehisi Coates reminds us, this is our world, and we have to find a way to live within it; as Ezekiel Kweku adds, working through despair might provide us with nearly unlimited will, because we'll no longer be afraid of losing. And, finally, as Toni

Morrison exhorted from the pages of *The Nation* in 2015, a time of dread is "precisely the time when artists go to work. There is no time for despair, no place for self-pity, no need for silence, no room for fear. We speak, we write, we do language. That is how civilizations heal." And this, in our own different ways, is how we all might heal. We move forward by doing what we do best, but finding new ways to do it together.

So a few thoughts about the path forward, about the things we might do. As I noted across the book, creating a more generous environment in which we can work together toward a new public commitment to higher education is going to require us all—from the individual level up through the institutional—to step outside the structures of competition into which we've been led and instead find new ways to approach problems together, in solidarity with one another. Taking that step at the university level, however, will mean that institutions must develop new structures that can support such collaboration, that can enable distributed teams to work toward shared goals, with common priorities and modes of evaluation. A few key projects that are emerging in libraries today might provide test beds for these new structures. The recent acquisition of several key pieces of scholarly communication infrastructure by particularly ravenous corporations—including the purchase of Mendeley, the Social Science Research Network, and bepress by Elsevier, and the purchase of Github by Microsoft—have encouraged a number of librarians to begin organizing around academy-owned infrastructure. Their goal is to ensure that libraries invest in and support projects that are collectively developed and collectively governed, which will in turn ensure that the projects continue to meet evolving library needs and continue to uphold core library values. But supporting such projects requires the individual libraries to place the needs of the collective alongside local needs, committing both funding and staff time to projects over which they cannot exercise full control or claim full ownership. Moreover, the distributed teams working on such projects—teams that are not only geographically dispersed but that also report to different administrative structures with different cultures and priorities—need to be supported in establishing goals and priorities that meet project needs even where they appear to conflict with local priorities. These teams—for an example, one might look at Samvera, an open-source, community-developed suite of repository systems—can provide compelling examples of the challenges that such collaborative projects face, but also of the real opportunities that collective action presents for solving problems in higher education. Those of us who work on campus need to explore these models, to think about the other kinds of problems that we might take on collectively, and to begin building the networks of support necessary to make such collaborations succeed.

Those networks of support are vital, not least because transformational change within universities and in the broader culture they serve—allowing all of us to return a focus on the public good—will require massive organization and mobilization. The social movements of the Progressive Era, of the 1930s, and of the 1960s demanded institutional and political change in order to ensure that the nation better live up to its responsibility for the public welfare. Today, movements including #BlackLivesMatter, #MeToo, and #MarchforOurLives are similarly demanding change in the face of stark opposition, calling attention to the violence carried out against black bodies by the visible and invisible structures of white supremacy, the violence enacted against women by the ingrained structures of misogyny, the violence terrorizing children in a culture that prizes individual liberties over and above the common good. These grassroots movements, gathering thousands upon thousands of protesters in demonstrations both online and off, model the power of organizing for social change, even—or perhaps especially—where the structural violences they call attention to give every impression of being too ingrained, too well-financed, too self-healing to be movable. This power has been demonstrated in the spring of 2018 through a wave of strikes in half a dozen states from West Virginia to Arizona as teachers walked out of their classrooms to protest declining real wages and deteriorating school conditions. And beyond the United States, such strikes have reached the university level, when, for instance, the University and College Union in the United Kingdom went on strike in response to dramatic cuts to the pension system. The significance of these strikes has extended beyond the particular locations and situations in which they've taken place; as labor historian Jon Shelton argues, it's possible that "striking teachers across the country represent the beginning of a trend in which the ordinary people who keep our education system—and our economy—running realize just how much power they have."

What is necessary to make such a realization possible, and to support that realization with the mobilization necessary to demonstrate that power? The interlibrary, interinstitutional collaborations that are developing around academy-owned infrastructure require a commitment to open, inclusive processes and practices, to collective priorities for decision-making, to ongoing discussion and reevaluation of project goals. The social movements that are gathering around us similarly require a commitment to solidarity, to listening, to learning. In both cases, these collective processes ask us all to honor new forms of leadership. And they also ask us to show up and do the work.

The political and institutional obstacles in front of us, the blockages that prevent us from creating the kinds of universities that might be communities, that might support communities, are huge. Our thinking must be equally so. And that requires all of us to think beyond our local allegiances, beyond our own situations, and to develop new forms of solidarity, of commitment, to one another. What does this mean? It means that tenured faculty must recognize their responsibility for the circumstances of adjuncts, both in allowing the current conditions to develop and in shaping the possibilities that the future might hold. It means that faculty generally must shake off the hierarchical distinctions that separate them from administrative and support staff: we are all laborers in the same enterprise. And it means that those of us on campus must find ways to make the borders that separate us from the communities off campus more permeable, enabling the university to become a center where those communities—our communities—can organize.

This is generous thinking: listening to one another, recognizing that we have as much to learn as we do to teach, finding ways to use our collective knowledge for the public good. From the broadest rethinking of our political and institutional landscape, to developing new ways of working in public, to sharing our ways of reading, to focusing on the most intimate practice of listening—at each level, we must be connected to, fully part of, the world around us. The university has the potential to model a more generous public sphere, but only if each of us—faculty, staff, students, parents, policy makers, and everyone who cares about the future of higher education—takes up that charge. As I told my students in 2004, recent events do not give me hope, but they do give me purpose.

But these last thoughts merely scratch the surface of what can and should be done; the longer I've worked on this project, the more I've recognized that "okay, so what do we *do?*" is a question that is going to require more minds than mine to answer. In February 2018, I posted the first draft of this book online for community review and feedback, in no small part because I knew how limited my own vision was. The discussion that ensued and that strongly influenced the book you have read remains available at http://generousthinking.hcommons.org. I hope that our discussion might continue there. Please visit, respond, and share your own ideas for the path forward.

Acknowledgments

A project like this one, which seeks to build a community, requires a community to come to fruition. I owe many debts to that community, but my first thanks are due to Lucretia McCulley, Rob Nelson, Kevin Butterfield, Nicole Sackley, and their many colleagues at the University of Richmond, for inviting me to visit. The talk I gave there in February 2016 turned out to be the first tentative steps toward this project, and their generous reception and engagement with the ideas I presented played an enormous role in its development. I am likewise grateful to Dan Anderson at the University of North Carolina, Ed Cohn at Grinnell College, Richard Ekman and Philip Katz of the Council of Independent Colleges, and Lisa Nakamura at the University of Michigan, all of whom gave me opportunities to present and discuss these ideas as they developed.

Enormous thanks as well go to the readers who participated in the community review process for the draft of this book: Rick Blackwood, Sheila Brennan, Steve Brier, Natalie Brown, Dan Cohen, Martin Paul Eve, Anke Finger, Barbara Fister, Angela Gibson, Jennifer Howard, Alan Jacobs, Annie Johnson, Rebecca Kennison, Kreigh Knerr, François Lachance, Sharon Leon, Christopher Long, Cameron Neylon, David Parry, William Plater, Dara Regaignon, Katina Rogers, Dorothea Salo, Danica Savonick, Elliott Shore, Erik Simpson, Erin Templeton, Brandon Walsh, and Ethan Watrall all pointed me in important directions and helped me see where I was going wrong. Colleagues and friends including Brian Croxall, Amanda French, Mike Furlough, Matt Gold, Shana Kimball, Matt Kirschenbaum, Kari Kraus, Bethany

Nowviskie, Stephen Ramsay, Jason Rhody, Lisa Rhody, Mark Sample, and Sarah Werner also read pieces of the manuscript and discussed the project's ideas with me in less formal ways. Their time, attention, and care are generous thinking in action.

I am especially grateful to my colleagues in the College of Arts & Letters at Michigan State University, and in particular to Chris Long, Bill Hart-Davidson, Sonja Fritsche, Scott Schopieray, Kristen Mapes, and Cara Cilano, whose support has been crucial to imagining possible paths forward in very difficult times. I also want to thank Dara Regaignon for writing alongside me, if virtually so, and providing the right mix of encouragement and concern at the right moments.

Thanks also to Nicky Agate, Eric Knappe, Ryan Williams, and Anne Donlon, past and present members of the Humanities Commons team, for helping build the community that made the review process possible. And I owe several debts to Christian Wach for his ongoing work on CommentPress, on which so much scholarly conversation relies.

Thanks, finally, to Greg Britton, whose Sunday evening email message first gave me the sense that I might be onto something here, to Catherine Goldstead, whose assistance and support of this project have encouraged it along the way, and to everyone associated with Johns Hopkins University Press who bent over backward to help make this book possible.

And, always, to Rick Blackwood, without whom none of it would make sense at all.

Earlier versions of portions of chapter 4 were originally published as "Giving It Away: Sharing and the Future of Scholarly Communication," in the *Journal of Scholarly Publishing*, vol. 43, no. 4 (2012).

References

Note: Where I have consulted ebooks in the course of this project, I have included "page" numbers as provided by my ebook reader in my in-line citations, as well as listing a total number of pages in my bibliographic references. This is a nonstandard practice, but it's my hope that this combination of markers might help a reader of a print edition estimate the location of the original reference if desired.

7 U.S. Code § 304. Legal Information Institute, Cornell Law School. https://www.law.cornell.edu/uscode/text/7/304.

"About." *Public Philosophy Journal.* http://publicphilosophyjournal.org/about/.

"About HuMetricsHSS." *HuMetricsHSS.* http://humetricshss.org/about-2/.

"About the OTW." *Organization for Transformative Works.* https://transformativeworks.org/.

American Academy of Arts and Sciences. "Job Satisfaction of Humanities Majors." *Humanities Indicators.* http://www.humanitiesIndicators.org/content/indicatorDoc.aspx?i=292.

Anderson, Benedict. *Imagined Communities: Reflections on the Origin and Spread of Nationalism.* Verso, 1991.

Appiah, Kwame Anthony. *Cosmopolitanism: Ethics in a World of Strangers.* W. W. Norton, 2006. Ebook, 283pp.

———. "2017 Presidential Address: Boundaries of Culture." Modern Language Association. http://mla.org/Convention/Convention-History/MLA-Presidential-Addresses/2016-20-Presidential-Addresses/2017-Presidential-Address.

"Apply to an Object Lessons Workshop." *Object Lessons.* http://objectsobjectsobjects.com/workshop/.

Arnold, Matthew. *Culture and Anarchy.* Oxford University Press, 2009.

Aubry, Timothy Richard. *Reading as Therapy: What Contemporary Fiction Does for Middle-Class Americans.* University of Iowa Press, 2011.

Avillez, André Rosenbaum de, Mark D. Fisher, Kris Klotz, and Christopher P. Long. "Public Philosophy and Philosophical Publics: Performative Publishing and the Cultivation of Community." *The Good Society* 24, no. 2 (2016): 118–45. doi:10.5325/goodsociety.24.2.0118.

Baker, Mishell. "*question answered, next dude steps up to mic* . . ."
@mishellbaker, May 30, 2018. https://twitter.com/mishellbaker/status
/1001833488079728642.

Barthes, Roland. *The Pleasure of the Text.* Hill and Wang, 1975.

Beam, Adam. "Kentucky Gov. Matt Bevin Wants State Colleges and Universities to Produce More Electrical Engineers and Less French Literature
Scholars." *US News & World Report,* January 29, 2016. https://www.usnews
.com/news/us/articles/2016-01-29/in-kentucky-a-push-for-engineers-over
-french-lit-scholars.

Beard, Mary. *Women & Power: A Manifesto.* Profile Books Ltd., 2017.

Berg, Maggie, and Barbara Seeber. *The Slow Professor: Challenging the Culture
of Speed in the Academy.* University of Toronto Press, 2016.

Bérubé, Michael. "2013 Presidential Address: How We Got Here." Modern
Language Association. https://www.mla.org/Convention/Convention
-History/MLA-Presidential-Addresses/2011-15-Presidential-Addresses/2013
-Presidential-Address.

Best, Stephen, and Sharon Marcus. "Surface Reading: An Introduction."
Representations 108, no. 1 (2009): 1–21.

Blackwood, Sarah. "Editing as Carework: The Gendered Labor of Public
Intellectuals." *Avidly,* June 6, 2014. http://avidly.lareviewofbooks.org/2014
/06/06/editing-as-carework-the-gendered-labor-of-public-intellectuals.

Blaser, Lucinda. "*Old Weather:* Approaching Collections from a Different
Angle." In *Crowdsourcing Our Cultural Heritage,* edited by Mia Ridge,
45–55. Ashgate, 2014.

Block, Peter. *Community: The Structure of Belonging,* 2nd ed. Berrett-Koehler
Publishers Inc., 2018. Ebook, 375pp.

Bloom, Paul. *Against Empathy: The Case for Rational Compassion.* Harper-
Collins, 2016. Ebook, 317pp.

Bosman, Julie. "Gov. Scott Walker's Higher Education Budget Ignites
Backlash." *New York Times,* February 16, 2015. https://www.nytimes.com
/2015/02/17/us/politics/scott-walker-university-wisconsin.html.

Bowen, William G., and Eugene M. Tobin. *Locus of Authority: The Evolution of
Faculty Roles in the Governance of Higher Education.* Princeton University
Press, 2015.

Bradbury, Kelly Susan. *Reimagining Popular Notions of American Intellectual-
ism: Literacy, Education, and Class.* Southern Illinois University Press, 2016.
Ebook, 259pp.

Brennan, Sheila. Untitled comment on "Public Scholarship." *Generous Thinking*, March 3, 2018. https://generousthinking.hcommons.org/4 -working-in-public/public-scholarship/#comment-297.

Brier, Stephen. Untitled comment on "Possibilities." *Generous Thinking*, March 4, 2018. https://generousthinking.hcommons.org/5-the-university /possibilities/#comment-305.

Brooks, Peter. *Reading for the Plot: Design and Intention in Narrative.* Harvard University Press, 1992.

Brooks, Peter, and Hilary Jewett, eds. *The Humanities and Public Life.* Fordham University Press, 2014.

Burke, Kenneth. "Literature as Equipment for Living." *The Philosophy of Literary Form: Studies in Symbolic Action*, 293–304. University of California Press, 1973.

Carstensen, Vernon. "The Origin and Early Development of the Wisconsin Idea." *Wisconsin Magazine of History* 39, no. 3 (1956): 181–88. http://content .wisconsinhistory.org/cdm/compoundobject/collection/wmh/id/20599 /show/20549.

Chafkin, Max. "Udacity's Sebastian Thrun, Godfather of Free Online Education, Changes Course." *Fast Company*, November 14, 2013. https:// www.fastcompany.com/3021473/udacity-sebastian-thrun-uphill-climb.

Chan, Leslie, Darius Cuplinskas, Michael Eisen, Fred Friend, Yana Genova, Jean-Claude Guédon, Melissa Hagemann, et al. "Budapest Open Access Initiative." Budapest Open Access Initiative, February 14, 2002. http://www .soros.org/openaccess/read.shtml.

Chodorow, Nancy. *The Reproduction of Mothering: Psychoanalysis and the Sociology of Gender*, 2nd ed. University of California Press, 1999.

Christensen, Clayton. "Disruptive Innovation." *Clayton Christensen*, July 10, 2012. http://www.claytonchristensen.com/key-concepts/.

"Citizen Scholars." Michigan State University. http://citizenscholars.msu.edu/.

Clinton, Hillary. "At AME General Conference, Hillary Clinton Calls for Action in Wake of Recent Shootings." *The Briefing*, July 8, 2016. http:// hillaryclinton.com/briefing/updates/2016/07/08/at-ame-general-conference -hillary-clinton-calls-for-action-in-wake-of-recent-shootings.

Coates, Ta-Nehisi. *Between the World and Me.* Random House, 2015. Ebook, 139pp.

Cole, Bruce. "What's Wrong with the Humanities?" *Public Discourse*, February 1, 2016. http://www.thepublicdiscourse.com/2016/02/16248.

"Concerted Thought, Collaborative Action (v.2)." *The Future of the Print Record,* April 24, 2017. https://printrecord.mla.hcommons.org/concerted -thought-collaborative-action-v-2/.

"Criticism of Wikipedia." *Wikipedia.* https://en.wikipedia.org/wiki/Criticism _of_Wikipedia. Accessed September 20, 2017.

Crow, Michael M., and William B. Dabars. *Designing the New American University.* Johns Hopkins University Press, 2015.

Davis, Jade. "Draft of Empathy Manifesto #1: Emerging Technologies (VR) or Technically Feeling." *Jade E. Davis, PhD,* May 22, 2018. http://jadedid.com /blog/2018/05/21/draft-of-empathy-manifesto-1-emerging-technologies-vr -or-technically-feeling/.

Delbanco, Andrew. *College: What It Was, Is, and Should Be.* Princeton University Press, 2012.

"Detroit Stories." Michigan State University. http://mispartanimpact.msu.edu /stories/detroit/index.html.

Díaz, Junot. "Under President Trump, Radical Hope Is Our Best Weapon." *The New Yorker,* November 21, 2016. https://www.newyorker.com /magazine/2016/11/21/under-president-trump-radical-hope-is-our-best -weapon.

"The Dresher Center." University of Maryland, Baltimore County. http:// dreshercenter.umbc.edu/.

During, Simon. "Stop Defending the Humanities." *Public Books,* March 1, 2014, http://www.publicbooks.org/nonfiction/stop-defending-the -humanities.

Ehrenreich, Barbara. *Bright-Sided: How the Relentless Promotion of Positive Thinking Has Undermined America.* Henry Holt, 2009. Ebook, 309pp.

Elbow, Peter. *Writing without Teachers,* 2nd ed. Oxford University Press, 1998.

"Engagement & Outreach." Mead Witter School of Music, University of Wisconsin–Madison. http://www.music.wisc.edu/outreach/.

Ettarh, Fobazi. "Vocational Awe and Librarianship: The Lies We Tell Ourselves." *In the Library with the Lead Pipe,* January 10, 2018. http:// inthelibrarywiththeleadpipe.org/2018/vocational-awe/.

Eve, Martin Paul. *Literature against Criticism: University English and Con- temporary Fiction in Conflict.* Open Book Publishers, 2016.

———. "Open Publication, Digital Abundance, and Scarce Labour." *Journal of Scholarly Publishing* 49, no. 1 (2017): 26–40. doi:10.3138/jsp.49.1.26.

Fabricant, Michael, and Stephen Brier. *Austerity Blues: Fighting for the Soul of Public Higher Education.* Johns Hopkins University Press, 2016.

Felski, Rita. *The Limits of Critique.* University of Chicago Press, 2015. Ebook, 287pp.

———. *Uses of Literature.* Blackwell Publishing, 2008.

Ferguson, Roderick A. *We Demand: The University and Student Protests.* University of California Press, 2017.

Fischer, Suzanne. "A Hawaiian-Oakland Collaboration." *Oakland Museum of California,* August 20, 2015. http://museumca.org/story/hawaiian-oakland -collaboration.

Fister, Barbara. "'Reading as a Contact Sport': Online Book Groups and the Social Dimensions of Reading." *Babel Fish Bouillabaisse.* PressBooks, 2015. https://barbarafister.pressbooks.com/chapter/reading-as-a-contact-sport -online-book-groups-and-the-social-dimensions-of-reading/.

———. Untitled comment on "Public Engagement." *Generous Thinking,* March 1, 2018. https://generousthinking.hcommons.org/4-working-in -public/public-engagement/#comment-264.

Fitzpatrick, Kathleen. "Engage. Disengage. Repeat." *Kathleen Fitzpatrick,* October 20, 2013. http://kfitz.info/engage-disengage-repeat/.

Fitzpatrick, Kathleen, and Avi Santo. "Open Review: A Study of Contexts and Practices." MediaCommons, December 2012. http://mcpress.media -commons.org/open-review/.

Fluck, Winfried. "The Modernity of America and the Practice of Scholar-ship." In *Rethinking American History in a Global Age,* edited by Thomas Bender, 343–66. University of California Press, 2002.

Fraser, Nancy. "Rethinking the Public Sphere: A Contribution to the Critique of Actually Existing Democracy." *Social Text,* no. 25/26 (1990): 56–80.

Gargouri, Yassine, Chawki Hajjem, Vincent Larivière, Yves Gingras, Les Carr, Tim Brody, and Stevan Harnad. "Self-Selected or Mandated, Open Access Increases Citation Impact for Higher Quality Research." *PLOS ONE 5,* no. 10 (2010): e13636. doi:10.1371/journal.pone.0013636.

Gaulé, Patrick, and Nicolas Maystre. "Getting Cited: Does Open Access Help?" *Research Policy* 40, no. 10 (2011): 1332–38. doi:10.1016/j. respol.2011.05.025.

Gere, Anne Ruggles. *Intimate Practices: Literacy and Cultural Work in U.S. Women's Clubs, 1880–1920.* University of Illinois Press, 1997.

Gilligan, Carol. *In a Different Voice.* Harvard University Press, 1982.

Graff, Gerald. *Professing Literature: An Institutional History.* University of Chicago Press, 1989.

Grant, Adam. *Give and Take: Why Helping Others Drives Our Success.* Penguin Books, 2013.

Grant, Adam, and Reb Rebele. "Beat Generosity Burnout." *Harvard Business Review,* January 2017. http://hbr.org/2017/01/beat-generosity-burnout.

"Great World Texts." University of Wisconsin–Madison Center for the Humanities. http://humanities.wisc.edu/great-world-texts.

Greif, Mark. "What's Wrong with Public Intellectuals?" *The Chronicle of Higher Education,* February 13, 2015. http://www.chronicle.com/article /Whats-Wrong-With-Public/189921.

Grele, Ronald J. "Whose Public? Whose History? What Is the Goal of a Public Historian?" *Public Historian* 3, no. 1 (1981): 40–48. doi:10.2307/ 3377160.

Guillory, John. "The Ethical Practice of Modernity: The Example of Reading." In *The Turn to Ethics,* edited by Marjorie Garber, Beatrice Hanssen, and Rebecca L. Walkowitz, 29–46. Routledge, 2000.

Hacking, Ian. "Introductory Essay." *The Structure of Scientific Revolutions* by Thomas S. Kuhn, 50th Anniversary ed. University of Chicago Press, 2012.

Harding, Sandra G. *Whose Science? Whose Knowledge? Thinking from Women's Lives.* Cornell University Press, 1991.

Harley, Diane, Sophia Krzys Acord, and C. Judson King. *Assessing the Future Landscape of Scholarly Communication: An Exploration of Faculty Values and Needs in Seven Disciplines.* Center for Studies in Higher Education, University of California, Berkeley, 2010.

Hathcock, April. "In a new working group and helped frame this norm: 'assume positive intent; own negative effects.'" @AprilHathcock, September 12, 2017. https://twitter.com/AprilHathcock/status/91094869818 7796484.

Hess, Amanda. "Is 'Empathy' Really What the Nation Needs?" *The New York Times Magazine,* November 29, 2016. https://www.nytimes.com/2016/11/29 /magazine/is-empathy-really-what-the-nation-needs.html.

Hitchcock, Steve. "The Effect of Open Access and Downloads ('Hits') on Citation Impact: A Bibliography of Studies." *The Open Citation Project,* June 25, 2013. http://opcit.eprints.org/oacitation-biblio.html.

Hitlin, Paul. *Research in the Crowdsourcing Age, a Case Study.* Pew Research Center, July 2016.

Hobson, Will, and Steven Rich. "Playing in the Red." *Washington Post,* November 23, 2015. http://www.washingtonpost.com/sf/sports/wp/2015 /11/23/running-up-the-bills/.

Hochschild, Arlie Russell. *Strangers in Their Own Land: Anger and Mourning on the American Right.* The New Press, 2016. Ebook, 511pp.

hooks, bell. *Teaching Community: A Pedagogy of Hope.* Routledge, 2003.

Horton, Myles, and Paulo Freire. *We Make the Road by Walking: Conversations on Education and Social Change,* edited by Brenda Bell, John Gaventa, and John Marshall Peters. Temple University Press, 1990.

"How to Prevent Nonprofit Employee Burnout." *Chronicle of Philanthropy,* http://philanthropy.com/resources/toolkit/how-to-prevent-nonprofit-emplo/93.

Howard, Rebecca Moore. "The Great Wall of African American Vernacular English in the American College Classroom." *JAC* 16, no. 2 (1996): 265–83. http://www.jstor.org/stable/20866079.

Hyde, Lewis. *The Gift: Creativity and the Artist in the Modern World.* Vintage Books, 2007. Ebook, 343pp.

"Improving Health Care through Technology and Research." Michigan State University College of Arts & Letters, August 10, 2017. http://www.cal.msu.edu/news/opel.

"Indigistory." *Indigistory.* http://www.indigistory.com/.

Jacobs, Alan. *How to Think: A Survival Guide for a World at Odds.* Currency, 2017.

———. *The Pleasures of Reading in an Age of Distraction.* Oxford University Press, 2011.

———. Untitled comment on "Generous Thinking." *Generous Thinking,* February 21, 2018. https://generousthinking.hcommons.org/1-introduction/generous-thinking/#comment-94.

———. "The Watchmen." *Harper's,* September 2016. https://harpers.org/archive/2016/09/the-watchmen/.

Jamison, Leslie. *The Empathy Exams.* Graywolf Press, 2014. Ebook, 234pp.

Joseph, Miranda. *Against the Romance of Community.* University of Minnesota Press, 2002.

Jurecic, Ann. "Empathy and the Critic." *College English* 74, no. 1 (2011): 10–27.

Kelber, Nathan. "Generous Thinking." Personal e-mail, December 23, 2017.

Kerr, Clark. *The Uses of the University,* 5th ed. Harvard University Press, 2001.

Klein, Amanda Ann, and Kristen Warner. "Erasing the Pop-Culture Scholar, One Click at a Time." *Chronicle of Higher Education,* July 6, 2016. http://www.chronicle.com/article/Erasing-the-Pop-Culture/237039.

Klein, Ezra. "Understanding Hillary." *Vox.com,* July 11, 2016. http://vox.com/a/hillary-clinton-interview/the-gap-listener-leadership-quality.

Klein, Lauren. "The Carework and Codework of the Digital Humanities." *Lauren Klein,* June 9, 2015. http://lklein.com/2015/06/the-carework-and -codework-of-the-digital-humanities.

Korhonen, Kuisma. "Textual Communities: Nancy, Blanchot, Derrida." *Culture Machines* 8 (2006). http://www.culturemachine.net/index.php/cm /article/viewArticle/35/43.

Kozlowski, Kim. "MSU Program Makes Detroit New Kind of Classroom." *Detroit News,* July 27, 2016. http://www.detroitnews.com/story/news/local /detroit-city/2016/07/27/msu-program-makes-detroit-new-kind-classroom /87647582/.

Krystal, Arthur. "The Novel as a Tool for Survival." *Chronicle of Higher Education,* March 6, 2016. http://www.chronicle.com/article/The-Novel-as -a-Tool-for/235565.

Kuhn, Thomas S. *The Structure of Scientific Revolutions,* 50th Anniversary ed. University of Chicago Press, 2012.

Kweku, Ezekiel. "Beyond Despair: Finding the Will to Fight Donald Trump." *MTV News,* February 13, 2017. http://mtv.com/news/2982785/beyond-despair.

LaCapra, Dominick. *History in Transit: Experience, Identity, Critical Theory.* Cornell University Press, 2004.

Lachance, François. Untitled comment on "Acts." *Generous Thinking,* March 11, 2018. https://generousthinking.hcommons.org/2-on-generosity /acts/#comment-354.

———. Untitled comment on "Paradigm Shift." *Generous Thinking,* March 17, 2018. https://generousthinking.hcommons.org/5-the-university/paradigm -shift/#comment-382.

Landsberg, Alison. *Prosthetic Memory: The Transformation of American Remembrance in the Age of Mass Culture.* Columbia University Press, 2004.

Latour, Bruno. *Reassembling the Social: An Introduction to Actor-Network-Theory.* Oxford University Press, 2005.

Leon, Sharon. Untitled comment on "Beyond Naive Reading." *Generous Thinking,* February 25, 2018. https://generousthinking.hcommons.org/3 -reading-together/beyond-naive-reading/#comment-151.

———. Untitled comment on "Public Intellectuals." *Generous Thinking,* February 25, 2018. https://generousthinking.hcommons.org/4-working-in -public/public-intellectuals/#comment-154.

Lipari, Lisbeth. *Listening, Thinking, Being: Toward an Ethics of Attunement.* Penn State University Press, 2014. Ebook, 566pp.

Long, Christopher. "Practicing Public Scholarship." *Public Philosophy Journal* 1, no. 1 (2017): 1–6. doi:10.1017/9781139628891.

Long, Elizabeth. *Book Clubs: Women and the Uses of Reading in Everyday Life.* University of Chicago Press, 2003.

Lubar, Steven. "Seven Rules for Public Humanists." *On Public Humanities,* June 5, 2014. https://stevenlubar.wordpress.com/2014/06/05/seven-rules-for -public-humanists/.

Lynch, Deirdre Shauna. *Loving Literature: A Cultural History.* University of Chicago Press, 2015. Ebook, 420pp.

Manguel, Alberto. *A History of Reading.* Penguin, 1996.

McAfee, Noëlle. "Public Knowledge." *Philosophy & Social Criticism* 30, no. 2 (2004): 139–57. doi:10.1177/0191453704041241.

McMillan Cottom, Tressie. "Academic Outrage: When the Culture Wars Go Digital." *Tressiemc,* July 7, 2017. https://tressiemc.com/essays-2/academic -outrage-when-the-culture-wars-go-digital.

———. "Finding Hope in a Loveless Place." *Tressiemc,* November 27, 2016. https://tressiemc.com/uncategorized/finding-hope-in-a-loveless-place.

———. *Lower Ed: The Troubling Rise of For-Profit Colleges in the New Economy.* The New Press, 2017.

"Mission, Humility & Conviction in Public Life." Humanities Institute, University of Connecticut. https://humilityandconviction.uconn.edu /blank/mission/.

Morrison, Toni. "No Place for Self-Pity, No Room for Fear." *The Nation,* March 23, 2015. https://www.thenation.com/article/no-place-self-pity-no -room-fear/.

Nancy, Jean-Luc. *Listening.* Translated by Charlotte Mandell. Fordham University Press, 2007.

National Humanities Alliance. *Study the Humanities: Make the Case,* 2018. https://www.studythehumanities.org/.

New York Public Library. "About." *What's on the Menu?* http://menus.nypl.org /about.

Newfield, Christopher. *The Great Mistake: How We Wrecked Public Universities and How We Can Fix Them.* Johns Hopkins University Press, 2016.

Newton, Derek. "It's Not Liberal Arts and Literature Majors Who Are Most Underemployed." *Forbes #OnCampus,* May 31, 2018. https://www.forbes .com/sites/dereknewton/2018/05/31/its-not-liberal-arts-and-literature -majors-who-are-most-underemployed/.

Nichols, Tom. *The Death of Expertise: The Campaign against Established Knowledge and Why It Matters.* Oxford University Press, 2017.

Noddings, Nel. *Caring: A Relational Approach to Ethics and Moral Education,* 2nd ed. University of California Press, 2013. Ebook, 351 pp.

Nowviskie, Bethany. "Digital Humanities in the Anthropocene." *Bethany Nowviskie,* July 10, 2014. nowviskie.org/2014/anthropocene.

Nussbaum, Martha Craven. *Not for Profit: Why Democracy Needs the Humanities.* Princeton University Press, 2010.

Okerson, Ann Shumelda, and James J. O'Donnell, eds. *Scholarly Journals at the Crossroads: A Subversive Proposal for Electronic Publishing.* Association of Research Libraries, 1995. http://hdl.handle.net/2027/mdp.39015034923758.

Oliveros, Pauline. *Deep Listening: A Composer's Sound Practice.* iUniverse, 2005.

Osborne, Robin. "Why Open Access Makes No Sense." In *Debating Open Access,* ed. Nigel Vincent and Chris Wickham, 96–105. British Academy, 2013.

Park, Clara Claiborne. *Rejoining the Common Reader: Essays, 1962–1990.* Northwestern University Press, 1991.

Parry, David. Untitled comment on "New Institutional Structures." *Planned Obsolescence: Publishing, Technology, and the Future of the Academy,* September 27, 2009. http://mcpress.media-commons.org/planned obsolescence/five-the-university/new-institutional-structures /#comment-85.

Perry, David M. "How Can We Untangle White Supremacy from Medieval Studies?" *Pacific Standard,* October 19, 2017. https://psmag.com/education /untangling-white-supremacy-from-medieval-studies.

Pippin, Robert. "In Defense of Naïve Reading." *Opinionator, New York Times,* October 10, 2010. http://opinionator.blogs.nytimes.com/2010/10/10/in -defense-of-naive-reading/.

Raddick, M. Jordan, Georgia Bracey, Pamela L. Gay, Chris J. Lintott, Phil Murray, Kevin Schawinski, Alexander S. Szalay, and Jan Vandenberg. "Galaxy Zoo: Exploring the Motivations of Citizen Science Volunteers." *Astronomy Education Review* 9, no. 1 (2010). doi:10.3847/AER2009036.

Radway, Janice A. *Reading the Romance: Women, Patriarchy, and Popular Literature.* University of North Carolina Press, 1984.

Readings, Bill. *The University in Ruins.* Harvard University Press, 1996.

Regaignon, Dara. Untitled comment on "Community." *Generous Thinking,* February 25, 2018. https://generousthinking.hcommons.org/5-the -university/community/#comment-185.

Rhody, Jason. "On 'The Value of Values' Workshop." *HuMetricsHSS*, November 15, 2017. http://humetricshss.org/blog/on-the-value-of-values-workshop-part-1/.

Rhody, Lisa. "What Can DHers Learn from Improvisation and Tina Fey?" *Lisa Rhody*, April 17, 2013. http://dayofdh2013.matrix.msu.edu/lmrhody/2013/04/17/what-can-dhers-learn-from-improvisation-and-tina-fey.

Ricoeur, Paul. *Freud and Philosophy: An Essay on Interpretation.* Yale University Press, 1970.

Ridge, Mia, ed. *Crowdsourcing Our Cultural Heritage.* Ashgate, 2014.

Robin, Corey. "How Intellectuals Create a Public." *Chronicle of Higher Education*, January 22, 2016. http://www.chronicle.com/article/How-Intellectuals-Create-a/234984.

Roth, Marco. "Tokens of Ruined Method." *n+1*, August 7, 2017. https://nplusonemag.com/issue-29/reviews/tokens-of-ruined-method/.

Roy Rosenzweig Center for History and New Media. "About." *The September 11 Digital Archive.* http://911digitalarchive.org/about.

Ruark, Jennifer. "Anatomy of a Hoax." *Chronicle of Higher Education*, January 1, 2017. http://www.chronicle.com/article/Anatomy-of-a-Hoax/238728.

Ruddick, Lisa. "When Nothing Is Cool." *Point Magazine*, December 7, 2015. https://thepointmag.com/2015/criticism/when-nothing-is-cool.

Salzberg, Steven. "Wisconsin Gov. Scott Walker's Dual Attacks on the University of Wisconsin." *Forbes*, June 12, 2015. https://www.forbes.com/sites/stevensalzberg/2015/06/12/wisconsin-gov-scott-walkers-dual-attacks-on-the-university-of-wisconsin/.

"Samvera." *Samvera.* https://samvera.org/.

Savonick, Danica. Untitled comment on "Generous Thinking." *Generous Thinking*, March 6, 2018. https://generousthinking.hcommons.org/1-introduction/generous-thinking/#comment-328.

Scholes, Robert. *The Crafty Reader.* Yale University Press, 2001.

Schonfeld, Roger C., and Ross Housewright. *Faculty Survey 2009: Key Strategic Insights for Libraries, Publishers, and Societies.* Ithaka S+R, 2010.

Schulz, Kathryn. *Being Wrong: Adventures in the Margin of Error.* Harper-Collins, 2010. Ebook, 598pp.

Scobey, David. "*E Pluribus Plenum:* Why We (the People) Need the Humanities." National Humanities Alliance Annual Meeting, March 2014.

Sedgwick, Eve Kosofsky. *Touching Feeling: Affect, Pedagogy, Performativity.* Duke University Press, 2003.

Shelton, Jon. "Teacher Strikes May Be More Powerful Now than Ever Before." *Washington Post*, April 4, 2018. https://www.washingtonpost.com/opinions /teacher-strikes-may-be-more-powerful-now-than-ever-before/2018/04/04 /d085bfb6-3767-11e8-acd5-35eac230e514_story.html.

Silbersweig, David. "A Harvard Medical School Professor Makes the Case for the Liberal Arts and Philosophy." *Washington Post*, December 24, 2015. https://www.washingtonpost.com/news/grade-point/wp/2015/12/24/a -harvard-medical-school-professor-makes-the-case-for-the-liberal-arts-and -philosophy.

Silverman, Jacob. "Against Enthusiasm." *Slate*, August 4, 2012. http://www .slate.com/articles/arts/books/2012/08/writers_and_readers_on_twitter _and_tumblr_we_need_more_criticism_less_liking_.html.

Simpson, Erik. Untitled comment on "Critique and Competition." *Generous Thinking*, March 23, 2018. https://generousthinking.hcommons.org/1 -introduction/critique-and-competition/#comment-395.

Small, Helen. *The Value of the Humanities.* Oxford University Press, 2013.

Sokal, Alan D. "Transgressing the Boundaries: Toward a Transformative Hermeneutics of Quantum Gravity." *Social Text*, no. 46/47 (Spring– Summer 1996): 217–52. doi:10.2307/466856.

Solnit, Rebecca. *Hope in the Dark: Untold Histories, Wild Possibilities*, updated ed. Haymarket Books, 2016. Ebook, 220pp.

Spivak, Gayatri Chakravorty. "Subaltern Studies: Deconstructing Historiography." In *Selected Subaltern Studies*, edited by Ranajit Guha and Gayatri Chakravorty Spivak, 3–32. Oxford University Press, 1988.

Stelter, Brian. "Oprah Calls and Reflects on 25 Years." *Media Decoder, New York Times*, May 24, 2011. http://mediadecoder.blogs.nytimes.com/2011/05 /24/oprah-calls-and-reflects-on-25-years/.

Stimpson, Catharine R. "Loving an Author, Loving a Text: Getting Love Back into the Humanities." *Confrontation* 104 (Summer 2009): 13–29.

Straub, Emma. "In Celebration of Enthusiasm." *Emma Straub's Life in Pictures*, August 3, 2012. http://emmastraub.tumblr.com/post/28643652265/in -celebration-of-enthusiasm.

Striphas, Ted. *The Late Age of Print: Everyday Book Culture from Consumerism to Control.* Columbia University Press, 2009.

Suber, Peter. *Open Access.* MIT Press, 2012. Ebook, 228pp.

Tchen, John Kuo Wei. "Creating a Dialogic Museum: The Chinatown History Museum Experiment." *Museums and Communities: The Politics of*

Public Culture, edited by Ivan Karp, Christine Mullen Kreamer, and Steven D. Lavine, 285–326. Smithsonian Institution Press, 1992.

Tippett, Krista. *Becoming Wise: An Inquiry into the Mystery and Art of Living*. Penguin, 2016. Ebook, 331pp.

"UniverCity Alliance." University of Wisconsin–Madison. https://univercity.wisc.edu/.

Van Hise, Charles. Untitled Address to the Press Association, February 1905. University of Wisconsin. https://www.wisc.edu/pdfs/VanHiseBeneficent Address.pdf.

Veblen, Thorstein. *The Theory of the Leisure Class*. Penguin, 1994.

Venuti, Lawrence. "How to Read a Translation." *Words without Borders*, July 2004. https://www.wordswithoutborders.org/article/how-to-read-a-translation.

Wallace, David Foster. *Infinite Jest*. Little, Brown and Company, 1996.

Watters, Audrey. "Ed-Tech in a Time of Trump." *Hack Education*, February 2, 2017. http://hackeducation.com/2017/02/02/ed-tech-and-trump.

———. "The Myth and the Millennialism of 'Disruptive Innovation.'" *Hack Education*, May 24, 2013. http://hackeducation.com/2013/05/24/disruptive-innovation.

Weil, Simone. "Letter to Joë Bousquet, 13 April 1942." *Cahiers du Sud*, no. 304 (1950): 421–23.

———. *Waiting for God*. HarperPerennial Modern Classics, 2009.

Wellmon, Chad. "After the University, Long Live the Academy!" *Chad Wellmon*, October 26, 2017. https://chadwellmon.com/2017/10/26/after-the-university-long-live-the-academy/.

"What We Believe." *Organization for Transformative Works*. http://www.transformativeworks.org/what_we_believe/.

Wolverton, Brad, et al. "Sports at Any Cost." *Huffington Post*, November 15, 2015. http://projects.huffingtonpost.com/ncaa/sports-at-any-cost.

Woodward, Kathleen. "The New Dissertation: Thinking Outside the (Proto-) Book." Modern Language Association Annual Convention, 2012. http://www.mla.org/program_details?prog_id=M025A.

Wurgaft, Benjamin Aldes. "The Call to Theory." *Revealer*, July 25, 2017. https://therevealer.org/the-call-to-theory/.

Young, Vershawn Ashanti. "'Nah, We Straight': An Argument against Code Switching." *JAC* 29, nos. 1–2 (2009): 49–76. http://www.jstor.org/stable/20866886.

Zahneis, Megan. "A College Considers Taking the 'Liberal' Out of 'Liberal Education.'" *Chronicle of Higher Education,* June 26, 2018. https://www.chronicle.com/article/A-College-Considers-Taking-the/243762.

Zwarg, Christina. *Feminist Conversations: Fuller, Emerson, and the Play of Reading.* Cornell University Press, 1995.

Index